Contents

*Affectionately dedicated to
Jeannine van der Voort
by the Steering Committee of the
Six Countries Programme*

INNOVATION POLICIES

An International Perspective

Edited by

GERRY SWEENEY

Frances Pinter Publishers Ltd. — London

© Six Countries Programme 1985

First published in 1985 by Frances Pinter (Publishers) Limited
25 Floral Street, London WC2E 9DS

British Library Cataloguing in Publication Data

Innovation policies: an international perspective.
  1. Technological innovation—Economic aspects
  I. Sweeney, Gerry
  338'.06   HC79.T4

ISBN 0-86187-574-5

Printed in Great Britain by SRP, Exeter

Introduction

The Six Countries Programme was established in 1974 following a series of UNECE meetings on innovation, at the instigation of Walter Zegveld of TNO, The Netherlands. During informal discussions at the UNECE meetings he found a common accord amongst colleagues from some other countries — the formal meetings of the formal inter-governmental organisations tended to make any statement a formal utterance of the Government represented. There was a need for change in thinking to tackle the problems of the future. He proposed a more informal group which, though still representative of government organisations, could examine and discuss freely policies and mechanisms to stimulate a higher level of innovative activity, especially in Europe. The result was the Four Countries Programme, consisting of organisations in France, Germany, the Netherlands and the United Kingdom. Canada and Ireland quickly joined and the Six Countries Programme was set on its course — not always an easy course because the programme was trying to develop its navigational aids as it progressed. Other countries have since joined — Belgium, Sweden and most recently Austria. The name, Six Countries, has been retained.

The Programme is ten years old. The Chapters of this book were written in 1984 to mark this anniversary, but much more they were written to mark a sense of attainment. The Six Countries Programme began its life with twice-yearly meetings of its members. Each was charged with study of some topic, but something was lacking. There was no synergy, the topics and studies were inert — interesting but not absorbing. A change was made to the holding of Workshops. Experts, researchers and experienced practitioners were brought together with the members of what had become the Steering Committee. The original objective was reached — frank representations of success and failures which led to further questioning. Many topics were tackled (a list is given at the end of this volume). Often the result seemed unsatisfactory. This or that mechanism did not work, or work in the way intended, or reach the target group. What then was the answer? Was there such a thing as an innovation policy? If there was, how could it be articulated? Could it be articulated as a formal government policy and implemented in formal programmes?

In November 1980, the questions which had been raised and remained disquieting were brought together at a Workshop in Berlin. The outcome was 'the systemic approach' which recognises the intensive interactions between all elements of society and the strong interdependencies between technology, economy and politics. Innovation policy if it is to be successful must take these into account. It must be not merely an articulated policy but an attitude of mind pervasive of all those formulating what are the implementing policies and pro-grammes — research, education, industry, information, en-vironment, manpower/employment, local government and finance. An innovation policy by creating a common attitude becomes the coordinating instrument, enabling each institution to perceive its role within the wider framework and creating a climate within which each can more favourably carry out its role.

The entrepreneur is the focal point of a systemic innovation policy. It is his investment in industrial innovation which creates economic wealth. Government can pick neither innovations nor projects nor winners. It cannot itself create wealth and there is no linear progression from research to innovation, from tax relief to creative use of technology or from other mechanisms to those entrepreneurial decisions which productively create wealth. Measures and programmes adopted should be so formulated and implemented that they provide direct and harmonious support to the entrepreneur. They only work when they stimulate the innovative drive of a multitude of entrepreneurs and a ferment of entrepreneurial activity.

Unfortunately, government response to the challenge of innovation has usually been to create an array of disparate mechanisms, administered by different Departments or Minis-ters rather than to address the much more complex task of systemic restructuring. Mechanisms are much more easy to comprehend and to administer within the public accountability system, but they may be self-cancelling in their effects or create further barriers. Stimulation of research in energy conservation may not result in new products because building regulations may inhibit their market. Large firms have the bureaucracy and the right choice of words to avail of tax reliefs, research grants and other mechanisms. Smaller firms, often the target group, face a plethora of bureaucrats and mechanisms. Removal of barriers to entrepreneurial vitality and investment in innovation is intrinsic to a systemic innovation policy.

Of the three elements which pervade the systemic approach to an innovation policy (see Gaudin, Chapter 2), the most difficult is the third, the creation of a technical culture. La culture technique sounds more mellifluous in the original French. Clumsy enough in English, it appears yet more difficult in other languages. Nevertheless, this concept is focussed on a vital need, the creation of an environment which will nourish both the entrepreneur and his innovative activities. The entrepreneur is an organic human being, and his activity is a product of his human creativity. The process of innovation is an organic, not a mechanistic one. It is a result both of culture and of culturing.

Since 1980, further discussion has amplified or provided further evidence to support the systemic approach. That it contains inherent difficulty for hierarchical and compartmentalised bureaucracies cannot be denied. Yet the evidence points in only this direction.

This present book is an attempt to bring some of this evidence and some of the Six Countries thinking to a wider public. Concern about the future, and its prospects for the younger generations, is widespread. The policies and mechanisms of the now old industrial age are no longer working. The change that is needed is a change primarily of attitude, of losing old concepts and gaining new ones. The reader will observe that each writer has approached his topic from his own viewpoint, but each is questioning established practices and indicating modes of supporting innovation. Each has been influenced by the systemic approach.

Credit for the generation of the concepts contained in this book must go not only to the contributors as contributors, but also to Walter Zegveld, god-father and first chairman of the Six Countries Programme, Thierry Gaudin second chairman and Helmar Krupp, who has so far avoided becoming chairman. Their influence and stimulus have led to this new approach. Many others have participated in the presentations and deliberations. To them the Six Countries Programme is grateful. To Dr. G. J. Wijers who contributed the first chapter to provide a setting for the more 'Six Countries' chapters, and to my colleague Michael Coghlan for his work on the texts of the contributors, the Editor is grateful.

G. P. Sweeney,
Editor and Chairman of Six Countries Programme.

CHAPTER 1

The Economic, Industrial and Institutional Setting

Dr. G. J. Wijers

Although he had not previously participated in the Programme Dr. Wijers was invited to provide a setting for innovation policy from an economist's viewpoint. He argues here for fundamental changes in societal institutions if Europe is not to shift permanently to the periphery of the world economy.

Dr. G. J. Wijers is a professional economist, specialising in macroeconomics and industrial organisation. Following a period as Associate Professor at Erasmus Universiteit in Rotterdam he was a senior adviser to the Dutch government in the fields of employment policy and technology policy. He is now working as senior adviser for Bakkenist, Spits & Co., Management Consultants, in Amsterdam.

Dr. Wijers is co-author of three books, one of them dealing with industrial policy (Industriepolitiek, Sterfert Kroes, Leiden, 1982) and he has published widely in the major Dutch economic journals.

1. Introduction

As 1984 draws to a close the western world is showing increasing optimism about the prospects for economic recovery. It is even suggested here and there that the long lasting period of economic stagnation since the first oil crisis has definitely come to an end. The tangible evidence for this opinion is the robust, persistent acceleration of economic growth in the U.S.A. and the modest revival in the economies of Japan and Europe.

In the following pages I will first try to answer the question whether there is indeed structural economic recovery in the western world. I will then look at the role of product and process innovation in economic growth. Finally the present technological— economic position and the prospects for the European economies will be analysed.

2.   Structural economic recovery?

1984 and 1985 could possibly show a continued growth of about 3% for the entire OECD area after a real growth of 4 to 5% in 1983.[1] These developments indeed suggest that there is structural economic recovery in the western world.

But is there? An economic recovery is only structural, if since the last crisis all supply-side factors experienced such a reallocation and/or technological transformation that they show a remunerative orientation for a longer period. In other words: the supply-side will have adjusted itself to such an extent that even during the fall of the business cycle some economic growth is possible.

Why then are there doubts about the structural character of the present recovery?

A detailed analysis of recent data shows that traditional Keynesian expansionary policies are the main reason for the present recovery. At least half of the growth in world trade in 1983 was caused by import growth in the U.S.A.[2] The expansionary policies that caused this growth resulted in a high budget deficit (about 200 billion in 1985). In combination with tight monetary policies this has led to a situation of extremely high interest rates. As the OECD rightly points out, this situation 'does not appear to be an auspicious starting point for the prolonged investment recovery, which would be required for a period of sustained, low-inflation growth'.[3]

The unstable situation in the U.S.A. influences the rest of the world economy in several ways. More and more third world countries, including newly industrialised countries like Brazil, are threatened by a negative downward spiral of high debts, enormous pay-off obligations, restrictive policies, less growth, less income, high debts etc. The resulting stagnation in that part of the world economy also means stagnation in several prospective markets for the industrialised countries, for instance in the sphere of capital goods.

The current, hesitant, recovery of the European economies is of course mainly caused by the expansion of world trade, resulting from American policies. The growth in several industries, like chemicals, is moreover influenced by a temporary advantage in price-competition, resulting from the strong dollar. On the other hand high interest rates in the U.S.A. keep European interest rates too high, discouraging investment and keeping budget deficits high. In the macro-economic forecasts for the European OECD countries the slightly more favourable expectations for economic growth are completely overshadowed by increasing unemployment rates (11.5% of the labour force at the end of 1985) and by stabilising or very slowly decreasing budget deficits.[4] In an economic sense Europe, of itself, hardly shows renewed dynamism, based on structural changes.

It is therefore hardly possible to speak of structural economic recovery in the Western world as a whole. In the U.S.A. the labour market, even at the height of the business cycle, is showing a substantial surplus of about 7.5%.[5] After the presidential elections taxes will go up or public expenditures will go down, probably resulting in less growth in the U.S.A. and stagnation again in Europe.

I believe that technological-institutional factors in particular provide an explanation for Europe's discouraging economic prospects.

3. Economic growth and technological development

The relationship between technological development and economic growth is very complex and has already been profoundly and extensively analysed by others.[6] In this short contribution I will restrict myself therefore to the line of approach offered by the concept of the product life cycle (plc).

The plc concept originally related only to the commercial development over time of one strictly defined product. Its meaning was later substantially extended by several authors. Vernon and Wells related the concept to international investments and trade streams.[7] Authors like de Jong and Utterback systematically described and analysed the dynamic interrelationship of the commercial development of a group of related products and the structure of the industry producing them.[8]

Table 1 gives a limited overview of the dynamics of structure, conduct and performance of an industry during the product life cycle. This is of course a very schematic overview, and in practice there are many exceptions to the suggested regularities in this frame of reference. Despite this the plc concept is more relevant than the sterile neo-classical models which are still so popular in economic science.

Table 1 shows that structural economic growth and employment are especially found in industries in the expansion and maturity phases of the lifecycle.

Countries with a fast growing economy are generally characterised by a sectoral structure with many industries in the first phases of the life cycle. What is more, industries pass very quickly through the different phases of the cycle.

Technology's role in all this is obvious. Groups of product innovations form the basis of new industries and as the development of a product goes further and reaches its limits, process innovations become more important. Diagram 1 shows these relations schematically.

In order to analyse the relationship between the plc concept and the structural economic problems of Europe, we have to consider the significance of the Kondratiev theory of long waves.

Following Schumpeter,[9] many authors[10] in the last few years have stressed the importance of the relationship between the diffusion of a new basic technology and a long wave in economic life with a periodicity of about 50 years. The diffusion process may not be that of one single basic technology but of a cluster of interrelated innovations in products, production

TABLE 1

The main characteristics of the product life-cycle theory

Phase:	Introduction	Expansion	Maturity	Stagnation
Structure	-production process relatively labour-intensive -production on a small scale -national, or regional market	-production process becomes more capital-intensive -vast expansion of production capacity -competition based on imitation -deconcentration -also export market	-production on big scale -product differentiation -high costs for promotion and service -oligopolistic market structure	-almost no possibilities left for price-competition -strong concentration tendencies -deinvestments
Conduct	-prepared to take high risks -both technical and commercial insight	-much attention to marketing and internal control	-much attention to consolidation of market shares	-tendency to coordinate company behaviour -attempts to buy young companies in expanding markets
Performance	-pre-operational losses -many failures -little employment	-substantial profits -substantial creation of employment -growth of exports	-declining profits -some disposal of labour -imports from other countries, loss of market share in export markets	-substantial company closures -substantial disposal of labour -further losses on international markets

Source: G. J. Wijers, Industriepolitiek, Leiden; Stenfert Kroese, 1982

DIAGRAM 1
The frequency of product and process innovations in the course of the product life cycle

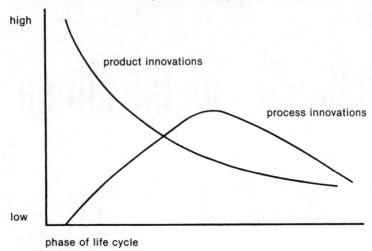

processes, materials and management methods.[11]

Besides the extensive process of renewal in these socio-economic variables, many societal institutions (law, education, government, etc.) show comparable radical changes. At a given moment this complete economic and institutional process of renewal comes to an end and a deep economic crisis develops.[12]

Perez has pointed out that such economic crises are caused, not so much by the absence of a new basic technology, as by a mismatch between such a technology and the societal institutions.[13]

Societal institutions happen to show a certain inertia when technical-economic processes demand radical changes. When the educational systems, the methods of management etc. of a country — or a group of countries — are still too strongly orientated towards the old technological paradigms, the cost advantages of the introduction of radical new technologies remain small and there will be no diffusion on a wide scale.

4.   The situation in Europe

The most important reason that the European economies in

general do not yet show signs of recovery is the rigidity of their institutions. It is observed by more and more authors that the focus of the new interesting economic activities is shifting away from the Atlantic to the Pacific region. The dominant multinational companies from the U.S.A. and Japan are investing less and less in Europe.[14] And the European multinationals are increasingly investing outside Europe. This development has undoubtedly contributed to the decreasing participation by the countries of the European Community in the trade in high technology products (Table 2).

TABLE 2

Specialisation coefficients for high technology products

	1963	1970	1980
EC	1.02	0.94	0.88
USA	1.29	1.27	1.20
Japan	0.56	0.87	1.41

Source: EC

Recent research by Booz-Allen and Hamilton[15] shows that this development is probably structural. The top managers of European companies themselves acknowledge that, contrary to the situation in the past, in not one important technology are European companies world leaders. The U.S.A. and to a lesser extent Japan have a big lead in manufacturing, robotics, computing, telecommunications, biotechnology and chemicals. According to the Booz-Allen research the most important reasons for this development are:

— the segmented market structure of Europe makes it difficult to capitalise the potential scale advantages of European markets;
— risk-taking and entrepreneurial behaviour are insufficiently stimulated by the fiscal, social and educational systems;
— compared to their Japanese and American colleagues, European managers tend to adopt a more defensive

strategy, oriented towards reducing costs instead of
stimulating product-innovations. And they have less
success in the process of commercialising new technologies.
— government policies are concentrated on the conservation
   of smokestack industries at the expense of stimulating new
   activities.

There is hardly any doubt that most of these factors are a
serious barrier to a wide diffusion of the technologies involved
in the 'information revolution'. This is an unacceptable
situation in view of Europe's existing problems with employment and economic growth.

To prevent a continuing shift by Europe to the periphery of
the world economy, radical institutional changes on a wide
scale are inescapable.

Freeman was quite right when he pointed out that these
changes will certainly not be the result of private market signals
only:[16] 'What is needed is not pre-Keynesian economics but
post-Keynesian economics'.

5.   Elements of a proposed post-Keynesian policy

Post-Keynesian economics implies quite a radical change in the
behaviour of governments, enterprises and other social-
economic institutions. It requires a vision about future society
that differs strongly from simple extrapolations. It is impossible
to describe these changes in detail in the short space of this
contribution. Therefore I will only propose several elements of
a post-Keynesian recovery policy.

Europe's potential in technological knowledge could be
better utilised if there were a European industrial policy leading
towards a more homogeneous internal market. In this respect
the development of European norms and standards for high
technology products and the abolition of custom-barriers
should have priority. Within the EEC coordinated procurement
policies could be developed. Pooling of funds of companies and
governments could help to overcome the present inability to
develop sufficient critical R & D mass in certain technologies.[17]

Much less than in the past governments will have to play the champion role in the conservation of established institutions. They should rather function as catalysts in the process of social innovation. For instance substantial sums will have to be spent on infrastructural projects with a 'technological multiplier',[18] in spite of serious restrictions in national budgets. Money will be needed to stimulate R & D, education and training (so-called intangible investments). But most of all national governments should stimulate flexibility in societal institutions, like universities, government departments etc.

Management methods also need various changes. Research for instance by Peters and Waterman[19] shows that the assumed positive scale effects of big companies are disappointing in practice. Smaller, looser organisational structures, with substantial influence by blue-collar workers and small middle-management and staff departments, are much more efficient. The information revolution indeed stimulates the development of such organisational structures.

The earlier mentioned Booz-Allen and Hamilton research shows that, compared to their American colleagues, European top managers spend relatively little time on R & D projects in their company and pay relatively little attention to the linkage of these projects with marketing. In future European top managers will have to spend much more time on the strategic role of technology in their company's future.

In the first pages of this contribution I referred to the unfavourable prospects for employment in Europe. It is my conviction that there is no traditional solution for Europe's unemployment. Precisely because of technological developments a new vision should be developed concerning the role of employment in future society. In this context Gershuny[20] rightly stresses the importance of all kinds of production in the self-service economy. The important role of the 'prosumer' in the information society is also underlined by Toffler.[21] It would certainly serve the European countries if they could develop a coherent vision about the informal economy, the need for redistribution of work and technological development. In the long run post-Keynesian policies based on such a vision will certainly show more positive effects than the currently fashionable neo-liberal programmes that offer hardly any insight into the necessary social innovations.

1. OECD, *Economic Outlook,* July 1984
2. Op. cit., p.7
3. Op. cit., pp. 73 — 74
4. Op. cit., p.14
5. Op. cit., p.78
6. Vlg. N. Rosenberg, 'Inside the Black Box', *Technology and Economics,* Cambridge 1982; C. Freeman, *The Economics of Industrial Innovation,* London 1982
7. R. Vernon, *International Investment and International Trade in the Product Cycle,* Quarterly Journal of economics, 1966, pp. 196 — 207. L. T. Wells, *The Product Life Cycle and International Trade,* Boston, 1972
8. H. W. de Jong, *Dynamische Markttheorie,* Leiden, 1981; J. M. Utterback, 'The Dynamics of Product and Process Innovation in Industry', in: C. T. Hill en J. M. Utterback, *Technological Innovation for a Dynamic Economy,* New York 1979
9. J. A. Schumpeter, *Business Cycle,* 2 vols., New York, 1939
10. J. J. van Duijn, *The long wave in economic life,* London, 1983; C. Freeman et al, *Unemployment and technical innovation,* London, 1982
11. N. Rosenberg, *Perspectives on technology,* Cambridge, 1976
12. C. Perez, 'Structural change and the assimilation of new technologies in econostems', *Futures,* October 1983
13. Op. cit.
14. W. Verwey, *Het geduld van de multinationals is op,* NRC-Handelsblad, 18 April 1984
15. Research commissioned by *The Wall Street Journal.* The most important results are printed in the edition of 31 January, 1984
16. C. Freeman, 'Long waves and technical innovation', paper presented at the conference "Technology and economic development", The Hague, 15 September 1983
17. cfi. M. Albert and R. J. Ball, *Towards European economic recovery in the 1980s,* European Parliament, Working Documents, 1983 — 1984, Brussels
18. Freeman, 1983, p.19
19. T. J. Peters and R. H. Waterman, *In search of excellence,* New York, 1982
20. J. Gershuny, *Social innovation and the division of labour,* Oxford, 1983
21. A. Toffler, *The third wave,* New York, 1980

CHAPTER 2

Definition of Innovation Policies

Thierry Gaudin

Thierry Gaudin originally qualified as a mining engineer and has spent the past 12 years assisting in the development of French innovation policy at the French Ministry of Industry. He is currently Head of the Forecasting and Evaluation Division. A former Chairman of the Six Countries Programme he is the author of a widely acclaimed study of institutional resistance to innovation, 'L'Écoute des Silences', and is retained by OECD as an expert on innovation.

Here he argues that in the design of economic policies, innovation policy must not be considered as something subsidiary, but as a prime component. He discusses the need for a systemic approach to innovation which will combine the development of a 'technical culture', support for innovators and the removal of institutional barriers. He suggests that if Europe is to keep pace with the U.S. and Japan it needs to develop a similar ability to define and implement major strategic programmes.

Innovation policy is of central relevance to most of the major economic issues of today. That it has not been so perceived is the result of incomplete understanding of the nature of innovation and of the role of government in relation to it. It is regarded by some as a leftover from the Sixties debate on science policy and by others as a mere vogue. Unfortunately because it is itself an evolutionary concept it is still incompletely understood even by those groups intuitively committed to it.

The study of innovation policies is often seen as a secondary manifestation of the contemporary argument between the 'free market' and the 'interventionist' ideologies. According to the 'free market' ideology the public sector intervenes excessively in economic life. Many of its actions hinder creativity and its opportunities for intervention should be severely curtailed. According to the second ideology the public sector on the contrary is increasingly obliged to correct the distortions resulting from imperfect functioning of the private sector market economy.

This major political cleavage is evident in almost all countries of the world today: the Tory and Labour parties in Great Britain, the Republicans and Democrats in the U.S.A., the right wing and left wing in France, the Christian Democrats and Social Democrats in Germany. Even in the Eastern European countries, in spite of the ubiquitous state party, a self-governing ideological current aimed at preserving the autonomy of small economic units is developing. Everywhere, the question is the same: more or less government?

The result is that when innovation policy is discussed the arguments used almost always have a strongly doctrinaire flavour. One might therefore expect that when governments change there should also be radical transformations in the policies implemented by government departments. In reality however the resulting shifts of influence, although real, are limited in scope, in the image of the changes of government themselves which usually result from the transfer of only a small percentage of votes. Indeed when governments attempt radical application of their doctrine they are usually forced by economic events to return to a more middle of the road stance within a few months.

The truth is, and one of the major contributions of the work of the Six Countries Programme is to have pointed it out, that the concept of innovation is considerably more complex than is reflected in either the free market or the regulatory ideology. To understand innovation it is necessary to have a systemic vision and a theory based on the experience of what exactly is involved in the phenomenon.

What is the systemic approach?

In the present context the approach consists of dispelling the fiction that the public sector is characterised by bureaucracy whereas private enterprise is the seat of sound competition. There are many examples of 'private' bureaucracies, in particular in the large conglomerates and conversely, of lively competition between public organisations. It is not the 'public' or 'private' legal status which determines the specific sytemic characteristics of the units, i.e. the degrees of freedom, the pressure to compete, the nature of the stakes, the viscosity of the environment, the relations between centre and periphery.

The systemic approach also consists of dispelling the other fiction that because the public sector has the mission of ensuring that the economy functions as well as possible it will necessarily remedy distortions without creating others even more serious. The public sector is far from monolithic and its self-awareness takes not one but many forms. It is subdivided into a large number of institutions which take decisions based on an incomplete perception of the whole system.

Expressed in more positive terms the systemic approach to innovation policy uses two main tools: analysis of the logic of agents and institutional analysis. The two types of analysis have much in common.

The first postulates that a situation can only be understood by mentally putting oneself in the place of each of the main agents and evaluating the issues and constraints through his eyes. Only in this way can the logic of his behaviour be understood. The second analysis postulates that institutions exist unto themselves, are relatively independent, have a language, a territory and even, so to say, a psyche. The relationships between men and institutions are so rich and complex that it can be asked whether it is the men that inhabit the institutions or the institutions that inhabit the men. Professor Krupp has pointed out, for example, that the argument between the free market and the interventionist political ideologies is often mirrored within the public service itself, depending on the role of the particular government ministry. The Finance Ministry in Germany traditionally tends to support the free market thesis, whereas the Ministry for Research and Technology tends to be interventionist. These positions are logical, given the respective roles of the ministries concerned.

Any innovation policy is in fact based on a theory of innovation, which may or may not be explicit. It is of course extremely difficult to demonstrate the validity of an innovation theory because of the social complexity of the phenomena being studied. Then too the subject is surrounded by myth, because innovation affects everyone and everyone thinks he knows what innovation is. Add to this the prejudices derived from economic ideology and institutional self-interest and one finds a great body of conflicting mythology diverting attention away from the small body of facts that tends to show what innovation really is.

Thus for instance many companies pretend to believe that innovation results from an idea conceived in a research laboratory, which is then developed by the design and market analysis departments and finally 'launched' by a process comparable to the launch of a rocket. This is the so-called 'linear' pattern which still underlies many policies.

Such a language is obviously aimed at serving as justification for the organisational chart of the company, whereas observation of the facts shows that the phenomenon is quite different: some innovations stem from suggestions from customers or suppliers, others are born in the technical and production departments and still others, a minority, actually do originate in the research departments. As for the so-called 'organisation' of the launching process, it is actually studded with internal struggles between the staff promoting the innovation and the remainder of the structure.

One of the most acute observers of innovation, Professor Roberts of MIT, accumulated a mass of data on internal company behaviour from which he was able to distinguish five different roles: those of inventor, entrepreneur, organiser, sponsor and information gatekeeper (the one who controls the flow of information). He points out that although the same agent may play several roles at once it should always be kept in mind that the roles themselves are distinct. Not to recognise this can lead to failure: everyone knows examples of an inventor who mistook himself for an entrepreneur; of an entrepreneur who neglected to heed the warnings of an organiser (often an accountant); of innovation stifled at birth due to the lack of a sufficiently high placed sponsor capable of shielding it during initial development; of a company which became barren due to a lack of circulation of information and knowhow.

The theory of innovation is evolutionary, always incomplete but adapting to the needs of each new era. Just as innovations themselves require considerable time to be adopted by society so the innovation theory will not win acceptance like a truth revealed to mankind and instantly inspiring conviction. Even in science, where allegedly hard scientific arguments are used to compare the validity of theories, experience has shown that the new paradigms, as T. S. Kuhn has pointed out, do not win out over the old ones until after a period of silence, hesitation or even polemics, necessary to change the mental habits of the scientists. The cases of the theory of relativity or plate tectonics are two recent examples where such a process could be observed. Thus the idea of a universal, instantaneous revelation which illuminates awareness like lightning illuminates a night sky is, with regard to innovation, a mythical idea, more closely related to the consciousness of an individual than to the slow progress of conviction in the social body.

Three other important observations arise from investigating the history of innovations.

The first, demonstrated by Shapero, is the role of displaced persons, i.e. persons who underwent a rupture in their personal or professional life. For instance, immigrant populations in all countries supply an above average share of entrepreneurs and innovators. This is true not only of the Central European immigrants to America between the two wars but also, more recently, of the returned colonials in France, the southern Italians in northern Italy, the East Germans in West Germany, the Palestinians in Jordan etc. In ancient Greece, the Metics (meaning 'those who came from afar') were immigrants who were not entitled to citizenship in Athens and were obliged to live at the edge of the city. It is said that these Metics were highly enterprising and managed to control a good share of trade in Athens. One became master of arms supplies, and was finally accepted as a citizen towards the end of his life. It should be remembered today that innovation is often garbed in strange colours or expressed with the accent of the immigrant. How many ideas have been rejected because the person bearing them didn't fit the mould? In institutions where everyone wears a mask and a uniform anything new is purely and simply ignored.

The second observation is the presence of small impassioned groups. Such groups are easily recognised in the history of art but attentive observation of the history of science and technology also shows that most genuinely new concepts were originated by the collective work of a small enthusiastic group - less than fifteen persons — which invented a new language over the years. The language is used for mutual recognition, ensuring internal cohesion and coherence of the analysis from the outside. A few months at the least and sometimes even a few years of regular meetings may be necessary to achieve a creative mode of existence and share a common passion. There is no innovation without passion.

The third observation is almost self-evident: the nature of the innovations depends on the culture from which they stem. If turn of the century Vienna gave birth to so many scientists, if modern physics, psychoanalysis and philosophy owe so much to this formerly brilliant capital, it is because in Vienna the level of culture was very high and the quality of education exceptional. If Japan has been able to catch up with and overtake western technologies, obtaining industrial performances envied by the rest of the world, it is by applying management methods based on small groups (quality circles) and by a very high level of education, since 95% of the Japanese arriving on the labour market have completed secondary school. The university system as well as in-plant adult education are also highly developed.

After stating these few elements of the theory (incomplete) of innovation, we can now ask ourselves what form a policy for innovation should take. In the course of a meeting of the Six Countries Programme in Berlin in 1980 it emerged that a very large number of the measures taken by governments in other areas had positive or negative effects on innovation. It would also appear that many of the so-called innovation policies prepared up to now do not have an innovative intent. They are designed more to maintain and perpetuate what already exists than to give the new generations the opportunity of expressing their creativity. This is true for instance of the educational system, slow to change its programmes and methods, insufficiently integrating the new technologies, more preoccupied with reproducing past knowledge than with preparing young people to develop their creative potential. This is also true of government contracts, often so rigidly bound in rules and specifications that they only allow the repetition of earlier contracts, as well as sharing the quotas among established suppliers instead of calling on new firms. It is to be wondered whether the so-called innovation policies established by government departments in most countries were merely an alibi covering a refusal to change the anti-innovative practices developed elsewhere by other government departments.

I will now look at some of the common elements in existing innovation policies to determine in what respects their original intentions have been subverted and suggest some ways in which modifications to these policies could better serve the development of creativity. I will examine the policies in a three part framework:

> support for innovators
> technical culture
> reduction of obstacles to innovation.

Support for Innovators

When a government wishes to establish a policy of innovation, the first thing which comes to mind is to contribute financial support to the innovators. The most widespread form is an aid reimbursable in case of success by payment of a few percent of the sales of the innovation for which the aid was given. In Britain, Sweden and France, this aid is administered by a non-govermental state agency. However the total sums devoted to aids amount at best to a few thousandths of GNP. Although they may be a solution to some situations, they cannot have a significant bearing on the industrial system as a whole.

To understand this it is again necessary to apply systemic reasoning: direct aids to companies give rise to three reactions which decrease their effects.

First of all the big companies tend to appropriate them to finance marginal projects which they do not subsequently support. This is particulary evident when administration of the aid is centralised. The comparison before and after the 1979 reform in France is eloquent in this regard. Before 1979 administration of the aid was centralised and more than two-thirds of it was captured by five major groups, which were even called the 'main subscribers'. The 1979 reform put an agency, the ANVAR, in charge of the aid (formerly administered by a ministry), then set up regional offices of this agency with freedom to decide on amounts up to 1 million FFs (150,000 dollars) per operation. After a year and a half the former proportions were reversed with two-thirds of the aid going to small companies and less than one-third to the major companies. From this it can be concluded that the way in which the aid is distributed is more important than its total amount.

Secondly it may happen that helping a company, particularly one with a dominant position on the market, discourages more active competitors, challengers, whose presence alone stimulates competition. As those who administer government aid are often conformist, they have a tendency to choose the dominant company rather than the challenger, in which case the aid, instead of spurring both companies, decreases competitive pressure and consequently competitiveness.

Thirdly, when the aid is handed out in small, homeopathic doses, it provides an excuse for the normal financing circuits not to take risks. When a case appears somewhat unusual, the banker directs it to the aids system and lets himself be guided by the reply. If the aid is refused he refuses his credit and if it is accepted he also accepts. This alibi effect means that aid has become a narrow door through which the innovator must necessarily pass, with no other alternative. If he is not able to make himself understood by the expert so much the worse for him. Everyone knows how prejudiced experts are and to what extent the NIH (not invented here) factor influences their judgement.

This tendency to mimicry is so powerful that the existence of an aid can actually restrict the flow of funding for innovation: if the amount of aid is stingy the prospects for venture funding are decreased.

What general conditions must be satisfied for the aids to be sufficient in spite of these three homeostatic reactions which tend to decrease or even cancel their effects? Consider the following diagram, illustrating what is customarily called the Rudder principle.

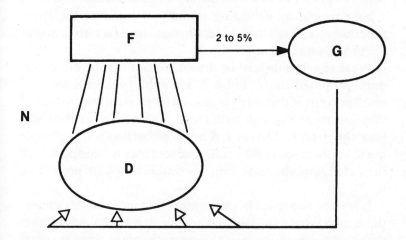

When a financing system F regularly supplies a number of receivers D a form of order is created according to the thermodynamic rules for dissipating systems (in this case, dissipating funds) set forth by Mr. Prigogine, that is a ritual of negotation N in which the arguments are invariable and the calculations made each year are based on those from the previous year. Many politicians, when arriving in government, believe that, they can substantially change the distribution of the flow of money between F and D. In practice they never do, unless they apply very authoritarian methods, because to do so would jeopardise the very existence of certain elements of D, as negotiation N concerns the survival of D. It generally uses reasoning ad absurdum.

However what is possible is to create a rudder G, that is a lateral financing system employing some 2 to 5 per cent of the flow F to D and managed differently according to more future-oriented views, in direct relation with the elements of D. More than 2% is necessary for th such financing to be non-negligible and less than 5% for it to be able to remain outside the argument ad absurdum concerning the survival of D, because, in administration of public monies, there is true freedom only for limited amounts.

Then if G is held firmly by a helmsman (possibly collective) with a clear and well informed view, it can act like the rudder of a boat which, by deflecting streams of water at the stern, progressively pivots the whole, whereas the flow F to D acts as the propulsion system.

What conclusions can be drawn concerning the aid procedures proposed above? Either it is possible to divert between 2 and 5 per cent of the state's industrial investment and the aids, if they are managed with rigour and without favouritism, can have the rudder effect; or it is not possible and it is preferable not to set them up, as their consequences may be the opposite of the stated aims: they may limit innovation instead of promoting it.

It may be remarked in this context that indirect aids such as those addressed to a pair (research centre + company) rather than to a company alone or to a research centre alone are more efficient because they create ties and allow better circulation of the know-how gained from the project. Contrary to general belief the main result of an aid is not the realisation of the innovation to which the aid was devoted but capitalisation on and possibly circulation of the know-how gained from the operation. The intellectual investment is essential whereas the physical investment is only a particular modality of what is to be produced. This becomes sf-evident when one considers how the areas destroyed physically during the Second World War were rebuilt.

Let us now consider indirect aid systems and some of the problems associated with them.

Many countries, taking the view that public servants are not particularly competent to handle industrial research proposals, prefer to set up systematic aids, generally fiscal. First in Japan, then in the U.S.A., followed by France, a quarter of the increase in research expenditures is financed by a tax reduction. However such provisions are unlikely to be very efficient for three reasons.

Companies do not base decisions concerning research on a 25% cost reimbursement. Confidence in the research is far more important. And in any case research per se is inexpensive compared to the downstream cost of developing and marketing the ideas it throws up.

The second reason is that tax laws are already so complicated that only the major companies, who can afford top flight tax specialists, can take full advantage of them, whereas investigations (U.S.A., N.S.F.) show that a dollar invested in research in a small company yields twenty-four times more results than in a large company. The first thing to be done to give a tax incentive to creativity for small companies is to simplify tax laws. The time saved by the entrepreneur with simpler tax laws will be devoted to his main activity, the creation of wealth.

The third reason is that the tax incentive is more likely to stimulate the imagination of accountants rather than of scientists. Companies will be tempted to describe as 'research' work which was not formerly included under that heading, giving an impression of an increase in expenditure for industrial research, to the great satisfaction of the government, whereas in reality nothing has changed.

Let us now examine the controversial question of venture capital. At the end of the 1960's, Europeans observed that specialised financing companies had sprung up on the other side of the Atlantic to support the growth of high tech industry, whereas European capital was reluctant to engage in such ventures. The Europeans figured that artifically creating innovation financing companies by a tax incentive would make it possible to find a sufficient supply of capital for innovative enterprises. But this was mistaking the sympton for the cause of the problem. Nothing is better suited to systemic analysis than the financing circuits, with such complex and sensitive reactions. In this case, the analysis of the American system was incomplete to begin with. Closer observation would have revealed that the term 'venture' used across the Atlantic had nothing 'venturous' but the name. The term actually covered operations set up for military contracts during the Vietnamese war. Although the techniques involved were state-of-the-art, they were supported by firm contracts awarded by the Secretary of Defense and the financial risk was therefore extremely limited. The situation of course changed afterwards when the companies converted to civil products. Then at the end of the 1970s, a genuine venture capital developed, buoyed by the expectation of huge markets for microelectronic products and biotechnologies.

Furthermore, American capital can afford a few years of venture in growing companies because of the prospect, in the over-the-counter market, of withdrawing when such companies enter the stock exchange. This allows the initial investor to get out in a reasonable time, which is not yet the case in Europe. Venture capital was therefore sluggish in Europe until the beginning of the 1980's when a few timid measures were taken to loosen up the financial markets (second market and mutual investment funds in France).

Here again, there was a confrontation between the free market and regulatory doctrines: the free market advocates claimed that venture capital was not taking risks because of excessive Government intervention on the money markets. This argument was obviously fallacious as the same capital was being used for even more venturous investments in real estate. Conversely, the defenders of regulatory doctrine claimed that it would on the contrary be sufficient for the money circuits to be in the hands of the Government for capital to be invested in long term ventures rather than speculation. This view was just as obviously unrealistic since the nationalised banks, already numerous in France before 1981, were not any more or any less venturous than private investment capital for reasons which become clear from a systemic analysis. And when the Government does request the nationalised banks to participate in derogatory financing, it is not always to support major technological ventures but instead to keep alive moribund companies and sectors, sometimes against all reason.

A system to supply sufficient capital for technological ventures must however be found. What does systemic analysis tell us?

It is not possible, as bankers are always reminding us, to ask a middleman to take risks in place of the owner of the capital. Ways must therefore be found to reestablish a direct contact between those who have the capital and the entrepreneurs. This contact must moreover be consistent with the new style of company being born, i.e. a molecular economy made up of tiny units built around the talent of a few persons. It could take on two forms.

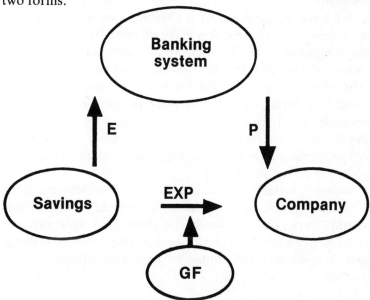

The first would be fiscal transparency of shares taken in new companies, or, to put it another way, the losses incurred during the would be deductible from taxable income. The efficiency of this provision, which exists in the American tax code, is widely recognised. It must be accompanied by deregulation of the stock market, as yet inaccessible to very small companies.

The second measure is participative savings, as illustrated on page 23

In the usual procedure, the person with savings places them in the bank system (arrow E), where they earn between 0 and 10% (disregarding special conditions offered on large deposits). The bank system then lends this money to companies (arrow P) at rates between 15 and 25%.

This gave rise to the idea that the person could lend his savings directly to company EXP, by a loan said to be participative as it is remunerated on the basis of the results of the company. To avoid excessive risk, a guarantee fund (of a type such as that managed by INODEV in France) would decrease the losses of the investor in the event of failure of the company.

What would happen if such a system were set up? Citizens would once again have stakes in the success of the ventures and the companies would be attentive to their image. Interest for industrial ventures and the new technologies would revive everywhere as a result of the direct contacts established.

All the forms of aid and incentive devised in various countries to promote innovation, stimulate venture capital, develop research, motivate the banks to finance risky ventures or spur companies into purchasing modern equipment could be passed in review in this way.

We felt it better to restrict ourselves to these three examples: direct aid reimbursable in case of success, tax incentive and venture capital, to show for the three cases how systemic reasoning can be used to X-ray the aids, give a non-naive image and even, within certain limits, to predict the effects.

Technical Culture

The concept of technical culture, on which is based the second aspect of innovation policies, gave rise to linguistic controversies within the Six Countries Programme. For the Swedes and the Germans, anything cultural is related to the arts and literature and is almost by definition different from what is technical. For the British, the conjunction of the two words is simply incongruous. In France, where the expression was born, it appeared provocative in the beginning, around 1978. It was perceived as a roundabout way of telling technicians that they lacked culture and cultured people that their culture was incomplete.

Despite these semantic problems the concept of technical culture has proved to be of positive value in discussing innovation policy.

'If you don't believe in knowledge, try ignorance' says an American company. To integrate technique into popular culture is to provide the means of recreating the technical world for the greatest number; what is going on today is only a feeble attempt.

The concept of technical culture is thus related to two ideas:

- the first is that in today's technical world, know-how is at least as important as knowledge.
- the second is that this know-how can be communicated to the population as a whole instead of being confiscated by specialists, thereby creating the conditions for popular reappropriation of technique.

But what is involved in a policy of technical culture?

Today, at the end of the twentieth century, after several decades of Fordism, we are witnessing a general movement towards intellectualisation of technique, the era foreseen by the futurist Gaston Berger, when he said: 'What is mechanical will be taken over by the machine'. The era opening before us is accompanied by an eruption of technical vocabulary. There are innumerable varieties of plastics, ceramics and composites. Computer languages are increasingly being enriched and biology is finding new species of organic molecules with poetic names (endorphines).

This intellectualisation places education, an area in which Japan has widened the gap in its favour, and more generally intellectual investment, at the forefront of competitiveness. As was said by a Japanese engineer, 'We have made a major effort for secondary education. The result is that the workers in the factories know what they are doing and why they are doing it, which does not always seem to be the case with you'. To anyone who examines this matter with any objectivity, it is clear that countries which set up a modernised secondary educational system for everyone in the 1980's will be able to claim mastery of technology in the year 2000 whereas the others will merely submit to it.

Each period of technical mutation brings with it a new series of winners and losers. The one we are living through is particularly radical. To understand it, it is necessary to go back in history. It has only recently become possible, folowing the works of B. Gille and Jean Gimpel, to establish an overall, although temporary, view according to which two periods of technical mutation comparable to the one we are living through occurred in the past. The first occurred during the Middle Ages, around the twelfth century; the second, at the end of the eighteenth century, is known under the name of 'industrial revolution', the beginning of the era of 'machinism'.

It is remarkable to observe to what extent these three technical 'revolutions' or mutations resemble each other. In all three cases, four generic transformations were at work concerning the same four transformational poles, i.e. materials, energy, relationship with the living and structuring of time.

In the Middle Ages, the agrarian revolution corresponds to: 1. the use of iron for farming implements (materials); 2. the erection of windmills as independent sources of energy (energy); 3. the selection of grains and animals (relationship with the living); 4. the construction of clocks on the bell towers of village churches (structuring of time).

In the 18th and 19th century, the industrial revolution

corresponds to: 1. the general use of steel and cement (materials); 2. the steam engine and the internal combustion engine (energy); 3. vaccination and Pasteur's microbiology (relationship with the living); 4. time studies, factory work and Taylorism (time structuring).

At present, it seems certain that we are living through a third revolution which could be called the revolution of intelligence. It corresponds to: 1. the use of polymers, elastomers and composites (materials); 2. electrical, nuclear and solar energy and energy conservation; 3. biotechnologies (relationship with the living); 4. microelectronics which, upon closer scrutiny, is nothing other than a new structuring of time.

The nature of modern electronics is in effect mastery of processes executed within a nanosecond (10^{-9} seconds). It is this mastery which allows very long programmes to be executed within a very short time, densifying complexity to an extent which simulates the living.

The year 1984, taken as a milestone by George Orwell, is undoubtedly the year 0 of the hallucinogen industry: artificial hearing (voice recognition), artificial sight (shape recognition), artificial image (drawn by a computer) and artificial sound (time-division switching, third generation telephone, laser disc) are arriving on the market simultaneously. Now that sight and hearing are affected by technology, it would not be reasonable to expect morals and social structures to remain unchanged. The future must now be imagined with the audacity of a science fiction author. Imagination must regain its rightful place in the middle of such rationalist down-to-earthness. Though clairvoyance regarding the future of technical civilisation may not be possible the recent history of microcomputers should be kept in mind. When the Apple II was introduced, nobody, including its promoters, believed that beyond the market of amateur computer fans, it would be such a rapid success with the general public. All the professional, including of course IBM, were unsparing of sarcasms for such a crude machine, which barely deserved the name of computer. In Silicon Valley, the leading firms are still saying, 'We were all dealt a severe blow by the success of microcomputer' and since 1979 they have all started producing them.

This shows that, where the instruments of the communication society are concerned, transformations are sometimes even more rapid than could be expected.

The second characteristic which must be kept in mind is that the present evolution has a cultural character. It affects sight, hearing, language and thus 'stirs the culture'.

In the old industrial countries, particularly in Europe, the continuing decline of coal, steel and the major manufacturing industries is a painful experience. This is the consequence of substitution of the new technical system where 'what is mechanical is taken over by the machine' for the old technical system of Taylorism, time studies and labour-intensive mass production industries. The local politicians ask what will replace the jobs that have disappeared. And everyone understands more or less confusedly, without daring to face up to it, that what will come as a replacement will not have much to do with what is being replaced.

It would be raising false hopes to lead workers to believe that declining industries will be replaced by other mass industries, more or less similar, capable of providing jobs for the large numbers of victims of the crisis after minimum reconversion, whereas it is no longer the large companies that are creating jobs but the small ones and the crafts. It is no longer the factories which are being developed but the third and even the fourth sectors, i.e. the industries of knowledge, arts and communication.

A genuine policy of technical culture, one which has not yet truly been implemented in any country, would consist of assuming this mutation on all levels. This is why the concept of technical culture is crucial to the many forms of government intervention.

It concerns the educational system, not only the number of years but also the contents of schooling. Are young people learning to use the new tools of the communication society: microcomputers, video, data banks? Most countries do have policies for providing the schools with microcomputers, but is the scale sufficient? In addition, the school system appears particularly rebellious to the idea of introducing video beyond the experimental stage, as video is a new language, more impressive, touching on the very matter of education. When will we in Europe have, like Japan, a TV channel entirely devoted to educational programmes?

As concerns higher, vocational and adult education, the concept of technical culture also involves both the content and the magnitude of the effort to be undertaken (in certain Japanese companies, engineers spend half their time in training as teachers or students): how does this apply to design, CAD, CAM, training in the creation of companies?

The Six Countries Progrmme was able to observe that networks of coordinators responsible for developing contacts between research and industry had been successfully set up in most countries. This is true of Germany, Sweden, Ireland, the Netherlands, Belgium, France, Britain. In the U.S., they are the 'industrial liaison officers' in contact with the universities; in Japan, they are in the 170 prefecture laboratories, responsible for providing technical support to small and medium sized companies. The usefulness of these coordinators is related to a cultural problem: the explosion of technical vocabulary isolates each person in his specialty, allowing enormous gaps in communication and comprehension to subsist. A language (English or French) includes some sixty thousand words. The richest authors use only five to six thousand words. However, the most complete technical inventories include some four and a half million items. Technology therefore represents approximately one hundred times the vocabulary of the usual language and one thousand times that of a cultivated man. What is the result? Linguistic isolates are created (trade vocabularies) where rule peremptory, touchy specialists, protecting their territory against incursions from the outside world.[1]

In France, an experiment demonstrated what cultural animation could contribute in a technical environment:

Microwave specialists were invited to work with meat processing specialists they did not know. The only common vocabulary both groups had in common was everyday language, but they were directed by an energetic coordinator who was charged with forcing them to explain themselves in a clear, functional language and preventing them from speaking their jargon. In one afternoon of this exercise, the group produced some twenty ideas for patents, which shows what creative effects communication between different linguistic fields can have.

To allow some coordinators to be fully efficient, they must form among themselves an interdisciplinary network. An isolated individual in an institution cannot help adopting the language and is not able to preserve his quality as translator except by regularly practising several jargons and remaining in contact with such a network of professional translators. Actually, these coordinators can be observed to organise local operations of all types and are genuine ferments of regional innovation policies. They are catalysers, crystallising initiatives, both for cooperation between firms and for setting up of research centres or other operations of the public sector.

On this subject, three remarks can be made in connection with the increasing complexity of technique:

The first is that the development of small and medium sized firms has reached a point where general technological services of a high professional quality and accessible at regional level are required, such as test and measurement facilities, access to documentation systems, collective research. The Japanese prefecture laboratories are a model. They include a total staff of 6,000 with highly diversified equipment.

How to finance such general technological services has given rise to doctrinaire debate. A variety of solutions have been adopted in different countries and often combine government financing, regional financing and contracts from industry. In certain cases, they are organisations of a more strictly professional character, such as the industrial technical centres in France, funded by levies.

Applying systemic reasoning to the particular issue of financing these services elicits two recommendations:

The first is not to reject complexity on principle. If various modes of funding are combined, this is the result of a process in which the diversity of the services rendered and the motivations are expressed. Simplification might appear esthetically satisfying, but this would also amount to denying nature of the ties established over time.

The second recommendation is that a systemic mode of financing can be imagined, corresponding to the needs of growth of this type of service. This consists of creating a quasi-market:

Let us imagine that it is decided at European level that all countries will adopt a tax provision called the 'one percent for

Technical research: decision-making levels and corresponding financing circuits

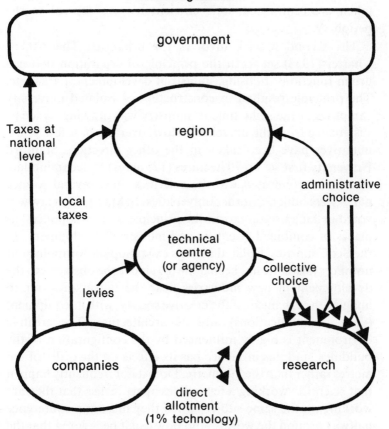

Quasi-market for technical research and general services

technology' according to which any company would be free to dispose of one percent of the added value tax which it would otherwise have paid to the State, providing this amount is spent in the reserch centre or technological institution of its choice (taken from a list of approved organisations). What would happen then? The companies would investigate the best way of spending this money, the technical laboratories and research centres, the engineering schools would attempt to be of use, the contacts between research and industry would be multiplied and a continuous state of progress and conviviality would be substituted for the lofty isolation into which each side now retires. Systemic analysis suggests that even when the iniatives taken are centralised, it is efficient to give control to the periphery.

The second remark involves the urbanists. The Athens Charter (1933) set forth the principle of separation between urban functions: housing, industrial development, parks, etc. The principle resulted in construction of isolated university campuses at the same time as industry was drawing its ideas, sustenance from the university. Now, over the past few years, initiatives have been taken in the other direction: Stanford University first set up 70 hectares (175 acres) to accommodate companies connected with its activities, then several science parks were built near other universities. In May 1983, a law was voted in Japan setting forth the principle of 'technopolises' as places of combined scientific and industrial development. In the Six Countries, isolated actions exist (Sophia Antipolis) but nothing systematic has been done to remove the obstacles to the development of new industries near the universities nor to imagine the urbanism of the creative society, with its equipment (data communications) and its architecture. The creative environment is highly influenced by the configuration of the buildings, and this influence has its effects on the order of ten metres rather than the kilometre. Does it not frequently happen that scientists working a few offices apart realise that they are working on the same subject when they meet at a conference halfway around the world? And how can it be ignored that the cubic cellular architecture of most university buildings erected over the last twenty years resembles Bentham's panoptic too closely to be conducive to creative thinking?

Third remark: when Japanese businessmen are asked about the reasons for their success, they mention the quality policy initiated in the 1950's and in particular the quality circles, small groups of some ten workers who regularly get together in the workshops to reflect on how to perfect what they are doing. The quality circles are characteristically a cultural device, taking into account the intellectualisation of the production process. What are they other than a method of disseminating intelligence down to the workshop level and involving all the hierarchical levels in reviewing production?

If one characteristic of the new technical system being established is predictable, it is that it will have 'distributed intelligence'. This is clearly seen when examining the evolution of computers and robots. The same is also true for social structures, as the difficulties in an increasingly complex system rapidly exceed the faculties of a single person, whatever his level of intelligence. Intellectual activity must therefore be distributed.

Future industry will undoubtedly be conceived by a few greatly talented men with a great technical culture. This can be see, for instance, in Silicon Valley, where the founders of companies are not only former brilliant academics but also experienced practitioners having worked in a large company on a specific technique for some ten years. At the same time, it can be said that this future industry will also be determined by the average level of qualification of the employees and their participation in the general progress. It is no longer sufficient to select, as is done for instance in France, super-elites and persuade them to leave their studies when they are 25 for management functions. In addition, they must acquire a thorough technical culture and a specialty, and the general level of the entire population must be raised.

The Obstacles to Innovation

The third aspect of innovation policies, one which has only

been touched on by Governments, is the reduction of the obstacles raised before the innovator or which hinder certain phases of the innovation process.

And why is such a policy now a necessity? Because of the change in the technical system: the corsets of the old system are obstacles to the establishment of the new and, delaying such establishment, may cause not only a decline in competitiveness but also social ills.

How can such obstacles be detected? By systemic analysis accompanied by an X-ray method which could be called 'innovation-audit'.

The resistance to this undertaking must not be under-estimated. In a period of crisis, each social category hangs on to the benefits it has won. The privileged attempt to consolidate their privileges. A strong political will is necessary to override the categorial or corporate interests. Everywhere, there are lobbies whose positions are called into question by the technical change.

In effect, industrial labour organisation is mainly charac-terised by task separation, as in the pin factory so well described by Adam Smith. The factory spirit, which is that of the division of labour, has penetrated the entire social fabric, including the third sector and even research. The result is that everyone considers his own the piece of territory on which he is exercising his competence, with the same attachment as was shown by the peasant for his fields in earlier times. Unfortunately, the existence of this territory is contingent on a given state of technique. When the technique changes, the territory dis-appears and the person concerned feels as though he has fallen into a vacuum.

It must be added that even when changes were predictable, they were rejected by those concerned: in Europe, the watchmaking industry was taken by surprise by the introduc-tion of the digital watch and the toy industry by microproces-sors and new materials. This was undoubtedly due to a lack of technical culture, but also to the understandable blindness of those who believed themselves to be in an impregnable fortress with their share of the market and their mastery of the distribution circuits fully protected.

Thus, the illusion that what appears solid is the sign of strong, lasting power remains a cultural feature inherited from the old technical system. For heavy industry and mass production, ownership of the production tools is the basis on which power is built. But, as this form of production declines, today a game of Monopoly is being played between different powers (capital, the State, trade unions) and the stakes are the modes of appropriation of these old tools.

Going back to the systemic point of view, it can be said that mankind was confronted with a particular form of complexity in each stage of its evolution. Agricultural complexity in the Middle Ages, with the diversity of species and the threat of diseases; industrial comlexity afterwards, with the abundance of raw materials and the diversity of processing modes; in all likelihood, the complexity with which mankind is confronted today is that of the mental universe: imagination, knowledge, or, as an economist would say, the immaterial, which is why the main resistances encountered in this area are mental rigidities (fostered of course by vested interests), obstacles to the fluidity of thought.

In a report to the U.S. Congress, Hannay, reviewing the functioning of the Food and Drug Administration, observed that in 1938, 27 pages were sufficient to make an application for marketing a new drug, whereas in 1976, the same application for a drug with fewer risks required 456 volumes and weighed no less than one ton. Upon hearing this report, Congress and American business went into a blind rage against the invasion of bureaucracy. A deregulation policy was applied to telecommunications, air transport and banking and was commenced for road transport, health and education.

It was no accident that the most positive results of deregulation were registered in the area of telecommunications, which is precisely at the crux of industries with a future. Each technique lives successively through phases of creative ferment and phases of consolidation and perfecting. Deregulation happened to come along exactly when the communication industries were entering a phase of creative ferment and it opened the door to let in the fresh air. The effect was entirely different for the airlines where, after a period of sounder management, it seems to have revived unbridled competition in a period when business was bad.

Here again, systemic analysis teaches us that the picture is not black and white. Deregulation operates well under certain circumstances but less well under others.

However, for Europe it is more than likely that the movement remains far short of what could have been done. What was the Treaty of Rome if not an effort towards community deregulation? And what is the situation today? Some twenty years later, there are still customs on the borders between the EEC countries! And the teamsters' strike is an opportune reminder of the absurd controls practiced on either side of the Mont Blanc tunnel.

More generally, it can be seen that forces tending to complicate the regulations are permanently at work. Each incident is the opportunity for them to pass new texts overlaid on the old like geological strata. The forces on the other side, opposing proliferous regulations and working towards simplification, appear weak by comparison. Even when official statements are made and clear stands are taken by governments, which may, as in Brazil, even involve the appointment of a minister responsible for debureaucratisation, these forces are working against odds of one to a thousand. They are confronted with a sort of entropy, a tide of small, molecular initiatives whose general result is always to make things more complicated.

In addition, there is not only official regulation. All institutions secrete, as they become structured, more or less implicit rules which become imposed by a sort of common law.

Thus, the company evaluation grid created by the banking system dates from the time when the ownership of machines, buildings and land was the basis of wealth. Today the banks are called upon to finance investments in intellectual or immaterial resources, which cannot be evaluated in the same way. The banking system is therefore constantly impeded by its calculation habits which are unsuitable for assessing the value of the brainwork incorporated in the operations.

Obstacles to innovation due to the practices of insurance companies, government contracts or the tax system could also be mentioned; each case would show a sedimentation of more or less visible rules, inherited from the old technical era and paralyzing the emergence of the new era.

In France, a report on the 'obstacles to expansion' was requested in 1960 of two 'wise men', Jacques Rueff and Louis Armand. After eight months of work involving several hundred experts, they had X-rayed not only the regulatory and bureaucratic obstacles, but also those due to the privileges of closed professions, which succeed in limiting the number of practitioners by various corporate measures: notaries, lawyers, taxi drivers, hairdressers and barbers, doctors, pharmacists, architects, etc. Twenty years later, the report has by no means lost its relevance: only a few of the obstacles mentioned have been eliminated although the rapporteurs not only identified them in 1960 but also proposed legal measures, inclusive of drafts of bills or decrees, in order to decrease them. This shows how difficult it is for governments to give precedence to the general interest over special interests. In 1981, the newsman Francois de Closets published in France the results of an investigation entitled 'Toujours plus' (Always more) when he described, using specific examples, how various social categories such as airline pilots use and abuse their negotiating strength to obtain exorbitant advantages, in certain cases paralysing sectors of the economy. His book shows all that remains to be done in the direction indicated by the Rueff-Armand report. In the final analysis, the real adversary of innovation is corporatism, not capitalism or socialism.

When structural rigidities prevent initiatives from being taken in the legal space, such initiatives take on another form: black market economy. Everyone is aware of the importance of this phenomenon in Italy and the revival of the innovative spirit to which it gave rise. The phenomenon is not however limited to Italy and is developing in all the European countries despite the protests of those who rightly consider themselves to be faced with unfair competition. When examined in the light of the innovation theory, the black market economy shows the way: it fits into the loopholes where something unplanned can be done, it upsets working hours, business codes, formalities of all types. It is the demonstration that where the code has become paralysing, it is inevitably circumvented and life always recovers its rights. It is nevertheless illegal, but it does show the way: instead of raising obstacles against moonlighting by regulations, would it not be better to adapt the regulations to the existence of moonlighting? Would this not be in accordance with the principle that law follows practice and adapts to its evolution?

The nature of innovation policies

A few main characteristics have come to light from this interrogation on the framework of innovation policies:

The innovation policy concerns most of the economic issues raised by governments. Do governments not feel responsible for changing their practices in order to solve the crisis? But in spite of the urgency, problems are not stated in terms of innovation policy. There are two reasons for this:

1. The theory of innovation and the systemic approach are conceptual tools which are not yet well known. Neglecting to apply the rigorous reasoning they require, the agents often prefer to take simplistic doctrinaire stands, either interventionist or free market.

The result is that innovation is often perceived as a romantic theme, surrounded by irrational legends glorifying individual creativity; in reality, the systemic analysis on which innovation policies are based is a *hyperrealistic* and *hyperrational* tool which instantly exposes most of the pretensions and hypocrisy behind which so many administrations conceal their intellectual laziness.

2. The logic of innovation policies means that they run up not only against mental habits and rigidities but also against vested or institutional interests which governments are wary of opposing.

During stable periods, there is a natural symbiosis between

governments and the lobbies which people society.

But it happens that we are living through an unstable period that combines rapid technical change with economic turbulence and crisis.

In Japanese, the word 'crisis' is expressed by juxtaposing two ideograms, the first meaning 'danger' and the second 'opportunity'. The message of this association of ideas is clear: danger for vested interests and opportunities for innovation. Often it proves necessary to choose between the two. Those who choose the first will make their country fall behind, whereas those who choose innovation will push it towards adventure, uncertainty and the unknown. This is what happens in times of turbulence. There is no easy choice.

This period is one where the decline of the great factories can only be compensated for by the creative ferment of small new companies. Governments thus have two main problems to solve:

— how to raise the level of technical culture of the entire population?
— how to make it possible to start a company without personal wealth?

Looking at the parts of the world where technology is growing, such as Silicon Valley and Japan, a general movement towards intellectualisation of industry can be seen, from which it can be concluded that in the future power will be based more on the activity of the mind and less on the accumulation of material wealth. The economic concepts must be revised accordingly. For instance, the concept of investment dear to Keynes is related to machines, buildings and land. It will now be necessary to also think in terms of intellectual investment, to give an economic, social and financial content to this new immaterial concept representing the accumulation of knowledge of all levels, from the quality circle in the factory up to fundamental research and refinement of investigation techniques.

Finally, innovation is a manifestation of life. It can be understood not by mechanistic schemes, but only by analogy with the living: gestation, germination, contagion are words which are relevant to the theory of innovation, whereas the mechanical metaphors so often used by economists such as weight, driving force, domain generally lead to mistaken conclusions.

The framework of innovation policies can thus be described by analogy with agriculture:

> Support for innovators: watering plants, giving them fertilizer
> Technical culture: ploughing the fields
> The reduction of obstacles: weeding.

One of the recent seminars of the Six Countries was devoted to evaluating innovation policies. It was observed that evaluation tools were still underdeveloped and that generally innovation policies were as yet not satisfactorily evaluated.

It should become possible to detail their general form as evaluation results become available.

At a later seminar, another more fundamental idea was expressed, the idea that the concept of innovation was in itself a particularly pertinent evaluation tool that could be applied to organisations, regulations and all sorts of a practices. If a given practice, whatever its goals is subjected to an investigation hinging on a single question: what are the obstacles to innovation that it engenders? The hidden side of the institution and its resistance to change are revealed, which is enough to spur on evolution.

Considering things from the standpoint of innovation amounts in effect, to going towards what is upcoming, towards the movement attempting to uncover what is emerging. This is of course unbalancing to the narrow-minded technical bigotry, which based only on observation of what is, tends to indefinitely repeat it. Because of the great transformations that are taking place thinking based on innovation has become a necessity despite the provocation it offers to established interests with their tendency to remain everlastingly the same. It is however provocative for what, already there, has a tendency to everlastingly remain the same, convening it to the future.

Innovation Policies around the World

In this review of current innovation policies I started with the financial devices for aiding innovators (the measures that first attract the attention of neophyte governments). Then came the policy of technical culture, which, I suggested, has nowhere been developed with the necessary amplitude. Finally there was the reduction of obstacles, still a vital project, but one which, so far, has met with only partial success.

It becomes very clear from an examination of Japanese and U.S. policies, that this approach is of limited value unless integrated into an overall plan that has its roots in the very definition of economic policies.

The major U.S. military and space programmes have powered American technical and economic developments for the last twenty years. The phenomena of Highway 128, and later of Silicon Valley, are to a considerable extent the feedback of research carried out for these programmes.

The Japanese method, though more subtle, is no less efficient. When a civil servant at the MITI speaks of the function of his office in relation to industry he says 'We must first draw up a common perspective; financing and fiscal advantages follow'.[2] After a large number of consultations, the MITI posts a concrete objective such as 'the plant without workers in 1985' or 'the 5th generation computer in 1990, while realising that the achievement of the objectives is less important than the energies they mobilise and the learning processes they engender. Objectives are valuable, particularly as symbols.

There is another striking Japanese policy — education. The visitor cannot avoid the impression that everything is educative in Japan. Not only are courses long and stressful but even television and the life in the company are used as vehicles for teaching, for intellectual investment. The case of the United States is quite different: the Americans complain of the weakness of their secondary education which is not compensated for by highly developed higher education and research. In fact it seems that the United States is living as if it were still the melting pot and the refuge for all the talented persons trained elsewhere in the world. This was so between the two wars, and even after the Second World War when the U.S. benefited by an influx of intellectuals escaping from persecution in their own countries. But can they resist for any length of time an insufficient average level of education, a population divided by discrimination of knowledge?

The last aspect that must be noted in relation to Japan and the United States is the attitude to competition and cooperation. We know the function of the anti-trust laws and of deregulation in America. The situation in Japan is different: the Japanese, who are adepts in the martial arts, acknowledge without difficulty that competition follows certain rules. It is normal that companies should cooperate at certain times and should compete at others. The MITI has a regulatory function. It organises cooperation for research and then reestablishes competition at the right moment.

Towards a redefinition of economic policies

In the design of economic policies innovation policy must not be considered as something marginal or accessory. It is centrally concerned with the promotion of change and movement, in opposition to the inertia of the existing structure which always tends to be static, immobile and repetitive. It is concerned with a process of creative destruction[3] which is resisted by the defensive reflexes of the existing structure.

This is where we find the paradox of innovation policies: we may ask whether to juxtapose the two words 'policy' and 'innovation' is not to compare two notions which are fundamentally contradictory. Is not policy based on the defence of interests that already exist, is it not already too impregnated with protection of the existing situation to tolerate innovation, except in tiny proportions? Those who have had to defend the innovators from inside the administrative or political system know how well institutions are able to manoeuvre when they feel themselves threatened.

Yet it can be said that an innovation policy goes beyond the simple representation of political interests. Some people represent it as the difference between the politician, who represents, or arbitrates between, existing forces, and the statesman, who is a party to a project that transcends but is aware of them. I would go beyond the increasingly quaint vocabulary of nation-state politics: this is a matter of global concern, a level at which there is no government, or no government yet, and would rather call it the defence of the general interest. Of course, the person who conducts a policy of innovation is also defending certain interests, but they are the interests of persons who are not yet born, the interests of the children of our children.

A policy of innovation, as an economic, social and cultural policy, is organised around the three poles common to every system:

— the concrete pole, that of means
— the relational pole, that of interactions
— the structural pole, that which imposes an order or directional tendency.

To take the customary notation, the three poles can be placed in a triangle as follows:

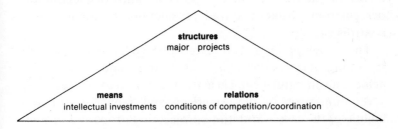

This pattern is valid at all levels: international, national, regional or company. In the case of a company, the base on which it operates — the basis of its wealth — is contained in the brains of its members and results from previous intellectual investment.[4] Complex relationships govern the interactions between individuals and their environment. Companies must therefore prepare a strategy of *intellectual investment.*

Competition and cooperation exist within companies in a number of forms. Individuals may become rivals, cliques may form, some relationships may evolve while others deteriorate. Unless clear thought is given to relationships and to defining equitable and methodical rules, a state of mind deveops that leads to unhealthy rivalry and to obsequious servility, with the result that energy that should be expressed in creation is wasted in conflict.

Whatever happens, the enterprise only really exists if it incarnates a project. Many believe that the only ambition of a company is to earn money. But money is only a means to the realisation of meaningful projects. How can one hope to motivate people if their work has not meaning other than in monetary symbols?

The three poles are illustrated at international or national level by the examples of the United States and Japan:

Intellectual investment generates a body of knowledge and of knowhow — it illustrates the policy of technical culture in all its aspects including research and education. *Conditions of cooperation and competition* are governed by the economic 'rules of the game' that comprise the policy of reducing obstacles (the Rueff Armand report), the anti-trust legislation, deregulation, obstacles to trade, freedom of installation, price controls etc.

The *major projects* have often obeyed military necessity (revealing an international inability to transcend rivalry and to achieve meaningful technical activity common to all countries).

A comparison of the American and Japanese strategies highlights the lack of ambitious projects in Europe and strongly suggests that this former cradle of technology is resigning itself to an inevitable decline.

Recommendations for Europe

Faced with the American and above all the Japanese policies, action in Europe is still very weak. That a project like ESPRIT should be considered a great success, in spite of the modest resources devoted to it and when compared with the stakes involved, is a sympton of European failure to pursue a policy that might threaten the principle of state sovereignty. This is a bizarre situation since national sovereignty is nowadays largely a fiction. Governments clutching outdated symbols are carried along by decisions that are taken elsewhere. They fail to control the multinationals —and it seems that every company now is founded with the object of becoming a multinational.

To replace a tottering national sovereignty, perhaps a European sovereignty could exist if an economic policy were drawn up on the basis of innovation, embracing:

1. intellectual investment, that is, not only thorough fundamental research but a policy of technical culture and extension of secondary education to the whole population (within about ten years).

2. a supplementary effort for deregulaton (the European Rueff-Armand report) and decentralisation (the Europe of regions).

3. the elaboration of a common intention — that of a creative society, combining art, teaching and industry and implementing the relevant major projects: information technology and space.

The Europeans could well promote a similar scheme on the world scale on the basis that the technological transformation at the end of the twentieth century involves intellectualisation of the production process, given that:

1. educational programmes throughout the world are under-sized or unsuitable (except perhaps in Japan) as is the dissemination of technical culture which would be carried out by use of the new media (satellites or direct television).

2. competition and cooperation must be reviewed from the European viewpoint, that is, respecting the diversity of cultures.

3. the present major work projects are entirely military, i.e. designed for destruction, which is staggering when a significant and consistent project of major works could launch an economic revival.[5]

EUROPE (at present)
major programmes
(limited scope)

space

intellectual investment   *cooperation and competition*
cultural   The common market
diversity   technical obstacles
education

THE UNITED STATES

major programmes
defence
NASA

intellectual investment   *cooperation and competition*
fundamental research   anti-trust laws
weak education facilities   deregulation

JAPAN

major programmes
a common overall perspective
the society of communication
INS (telecomm)
5th generation computers

intellectual investment   *competition and coordination*
higher education   controlled by MITI
old technologies and
communication facilities

EUROPE (potential)

major programmes
a common perspective
a creative society
information technology
space

intellectual investment	*cooperation and competition*
secondary technical	decentralisation
culture for all	deregulation

[1]The 200 words of the management language are undoubtedly the last, ridiculous attempt to reduce industrial reality to a paltry, normative vocabulary.

[2]We know only too well in Europe what happens when financing precedes planning: companies are supported not for the value of their plans and of their projects but on account of their difficulties, to 'save' jobs, often to the point of absurdity. In certain regions jobs have been 'saved' five or six times in the same year and one cannot help feeling that the relation of saver and saved that is established surreptitiously between government and companies, indefinitely reproduces a scenario of messianic inspiration in which everybody is looking backwards.

The main elements of European strategy that do incarnate forward-looking perspectives are the so-called 'major' programmes: space, telephone, nuclear, aeronautics, weapons, oceanography. Some have a positive image and others negative, but they all correspond to the same idea of a strategic viewpoint implemented by a powerful and organised apparatus.

[3]Schumpeter spoke of 'devastating and beneficial tempests' —although the adjective 'beneficial' may be excessive.

[4]The mistake is often made of believing that abilities can be bought and transplanted. This is not so — transplantations can be fecund but may also be sterile.

[5]See proposals made by Mr. Nagakima of the Mitsubishi Research Institute.

CHAPTER 3

Public Promotion of Innovation — Disappointments and Hopes

Helmar Krupp

Even when they are alleging the contrary governments in OECD countries have persistently intervened in the market in order to promote innovation in strategic areas. But the priorities selected today, in West Germany and elsewhere, are unlikely to yield a solution to the two major problems of unemployment and environmental deterioration. Professor Krupp argues that a concentration on efficient resource management offers the best prospect of increased employment, but will require a thoroughly integrated approach to policy formulation.

Professor Krupp is Director of the Institute for Systems Analysis and Innovation Research (ISI), Karlsruhe. He has more than two decades of experience in industrial science, first with the Hartmann and Braun company, Frankfurt, and later with the Batelle Institute, Frankfurt, where he was Director of the Department of Natural Sciences. He is a consultant to several national and international agencies including OECD, the European Commission and the German Ministry of Research and Technology. He has published widely both in the scientific field and on the theory of innovation policy.

Summary

After the last war all of our governments subscribed to the market doctrine according to which there should be no government intervention in the economy. This doctrine has been and still is being violated continuously, because it is neither realistic nor useful. In the Federal Republic of Germany, for example, the government heavily subsidised new industries for making atomic reactors, air and space vehicles. In all OECD countries innovation policies promoted advanced technologies by picking presumable winners. With reference to the market doctrine, however, indirect instruments of innovation policy (general grants and tax reliefs) are being applied recently, although they are probably less cost-effective than direct project funding provided that reasonable project selection and monitoring is achieved. In the past ten years small and medium-sized enterprises have become the main target of government promotion by means of a great variety of subsidies, including special funds, accommodation and infrastructure for the formation of new technology based enterprises. Again, the cost-effectiveness of some of these measures may be viewed critically.

Under the pressure of unemployment and fierce international competition all of our governments have developed a rich variety of innovation policies and measures. They have all concentrated on the promotion of the same so-called high technologies (space, micro-electronics and micro-optics, computers, automation, lasers, bio-technology etc.).

These innovation policies have been predominantly supply-oriented. Therefore, the main part of this paper is devoted to the elaboration of a complementary strategy of innovation which is more demand-oriented. It is argued that in the face of reduced growth rates, the present saturation of major consumer markets and, above all, the new situation of natural resources as well as the environmental predicaments, our innovation policies should place a high priority on increasing the productivity of our resources (energy, raw materials, water) including a reduction of the load on our environmental capacity. More generally, innovation policies should increase their attention to infrastructure and common goods, such as public transport, city renewal, quality of workplaces etc. In these sectors, matching of supply and demand is more indirect and demand has to be articulated and organised by public bodies. The main task of innovation policies in these areas is that of innovating the economic and legal conditions by appropriate de-and re-regulation. Thus, articulation and organisation of demand together with appropriate regulations would exert a demand pull on technologies to produce the desirable innovations efficiently.

This chapter ends with a glimpse into the present breathless competitive race among the quite protectionist OECD countries and it is suggested that the Six Countries Programme, in order to maintain its orientation towards the future, should include new policies in its deliberations which might also incorporate the Third World.

Introduction

1. The first part of this paper, in reviewing the evolution of post-war policies of technology and innovation, and our discussions thereof in the seminars of the Six Countries Programme, reveals that all our countries have subscribed to the same supply-oriented policies and the same fields of high technology. It seems useful, therefore, to ask whether we might complement our innovation policies by a second strategy, which is oriented to the pressing needs of our societies and which is therefore more demand-oriented. Such a second strategy is outlined in the second part of this paper.

The market doctrine and its violations

2. After the last war we experienced more than two decades of economic boom, unprecedented in history. High average growth rates prevailed, although modulated by periodic recessions every four to five years (Fig. 1). When our Six Countries 'Club' nucleated in Bucharest in 1972, we were still under the spell of these gay 50s and 60s. The basic policy, proposed in particular by our colleagues from ministries of economic affairs, was the *market doctrine* which stated:

Research and development (R & D) are part of the science system which provides a pool of general knowledge from which industry and government draw for their specific purposes. Research results constitute an undirected potential. It is in the hands of industry, primarily, that it becomes an innovative force directed towards specific products, processes and, finally, markets, including those under the responsibility of governments, such as education, health, transportation, armament, city renewal etc. It was quite logical, therefore, that in several countries and in different postwar periods the promulgation of R & D policies should have been assigned to ministries of culture and science.

3. In the Federal Republic of Germany this market doctrine, although officially still in use even today, was violated as early as 1955 by the formation of a Ministry for Atomic Energy. It created large national research centres and promoted industrial capacity to enable West Germany to become competitive in the field of atomic reactors. Starting in 1958, manufacturing of aircraft and space vehicles was triggered by similar government intervention (Braunling/Harmsen 1975). The same happened in other countries, for example the U.K. and France.

The process has been such that the list of R & D areas promoted by our governments has become quite long. All OECD countries now support ocean technology, micro-electronics, bio-technology, materials etc. Quite often, in spite of their large volume and specificity, these government grants for R & D have been defended, officially, by the argument that in themselves they are 'market neutral' because they are available to all companies, at least in principle. However, early in postwar technology policies it was recognised that innovation comes about by a close interaction between technology push and demand pull (Achilladelis et al. 1971; Nelson/Winter 1977). As a consequence, the cost effectiveness of R & D grants can be raised by focussing research onto the final product. In practice, this requires an intense involvement of industry even in the earliest stages of innovation.

This is being done in a variety of ways: by involving industry in the definition of government programmes, by grants in aid, by public procurement etc. For reasons of efficiency it cannot be done by involving all of industry or even all companies of a

FIGURE 1
Average growth rates of GNP in the Federal Republic of Germany

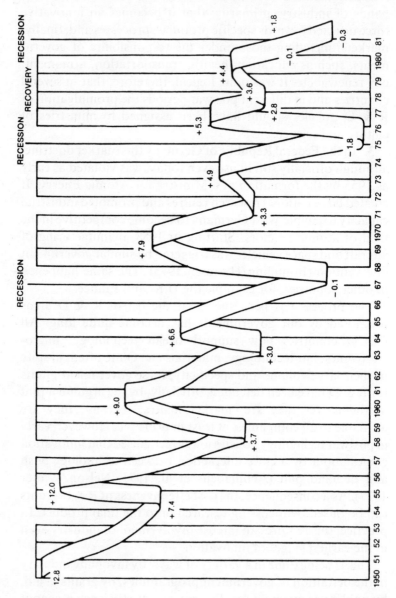

particular sector. Instead, individual companies or consortia of companies are being selected for support by government. These are the presumable winners within their sectors.

I conclude, therefore, that *efficient government support of innovation implies market intervention,* however cautiously it may be done. It is only in areas of fundamental research that intervention with industry may not be required.

4. Naturally, this government intervention in science, technology and markets, which is growing worldwide, met with criticism, for example, by our colleagues from SPRU, for example (Pavitt/Walker 1976, Nelson 1982). These critics were able to point at obvious failures: Hovercraft, SST (supersonic transport) and Concorde, the Clinch River breeder, the synfuel programme. Examples in West Germany are large computers, the magnetically suspended ultra-rapid train and our fast breeder reactor which may provide plutonium for bombs (Grupp et al. 1983) but is probably not needed for electricity production for at least a few decades (Keck 1981). The latest example of dubious selection of priorities for government R & D projects is the imminent construction of manned space stations under multinational participation. Discussion in the USA has shown that they may be useful for military purposes or as a political demonstration of strength but not for civilian objectives. Projects such as manufacturing in space, moon mining etc. serve big companies interested in large government contracts, but they do not have economical objectives, as shown by the lack of industrial response in Europe.

It is plausible that governments select large and long term projects for funding because only a few strong companies are interested in them and appropriate publicity can be organised to substitute for public support. By contrast, the shaping of shorter-term down-to-earth projects is complicated by the requirement that they must fit into the existing structures of competing industrial interests and markets. The controversies with respect to the forceful marketing of new media by the Federal Post Ministry are a recent example in the Federal Republic of Germany. They show the problems of direct government intervention, such as for example wrong project selection and inadequate project management (Keck 1981).

However, this example of telecommunication networks also shows that governments have an essential role to play in the innovation of such comprehensive national systems. This is discussed in the second part of this paper, from paragraph 20 onwards.

As a reaction, rather than abandoning market intervention, our countries now attempt to improve the mechanisms of project selection and management by cooperation of government and industry. In West Germany a recent key word for this is 'Verbundforschung' (combined research between industry and public R & D institutions supported by public funds). Unfortunately, this approach is not free from pitfalls. On the one hand, the cost effectiveness of such projects grows with demand pull and hence their closeness to competitive products and processes; on the other, so do the conflicting competitive interests of the companies involved. The inevitable compromise will reduce the cost-effectiveness of the projects. That is the reason why collective research in research associations has to adjust to some R & D level just above competitive interests and direct applicability. The resulting problem, how to transfer their R & D results effectively to potential users, is a familiar one (6CP Rothwell 1980).

Critical assessments seem to show that, because of the strength of their multinational corporations and the general political climate, the USA can afford to restrict its R & D policy to armaments and basic research. But our countries should not forgo wider public support for innovation.

In spite of setbacks, *direct aid,* provided that it is well managed, *seems to be the main and probably the most cost-effective instrument for governmental innovation policy.* Public procurement, as practised for armaments in the USA, may be a worthwhile alternative in particular fields. Regulation, discussed later, also has an important role.

5. About ten years ago, the debate in the Federal Republic of Germany focussed onto this general political issue in the following form:

It was conceded, particularly in the face of international

competition, that some amount of direct R & D funding of companies cannot be avoided. But influential and publicised opinion started to measure the quality of our ministers for research and technology by the ratio of their ministry's indirect over direct funding of industry. Indirect funding includes tax reliefs and grants to all or to particular classes of companies in proportion to their size or their R & D expenses etc. Many countries adopted such measures, but only in West Germany was this accompanied by an ideological debate on the relative merits of such indirect funding of R & D compared to direct funding of R & D projects. The futility of the debate may be demonstrated by the following quantitative argument: If from the budget of the German Ministry for Research and Technology we subtract the more or less fixed items (nuclear power, space, international projects, public R & D institutions etc.), the disposable budget is reduced to about 1 billion DM annually. There are about 10^5 companies of technical relevance in West Germany. If these disposable funds were distributed evenly among them, the resulting annual grants would amount to 10^4 DM per company. The effect of this sum on decisions and capabilities must be considered sub-threshold. In other words, indirect aid above threshold for all companies would be much more expensive than direct aid to the relevant companies for specific purposes. Thus, sub-threshold indirect aid can have only an effect on the general political climate, as it is called, or constitute symbolic politics, which — if appropriately designed and marketed — may be justified under particular circumstances.

Therefore, direct project funding within individual companies, on the one hand, and indirect funding of all relevant companies on the other are not comparable or interchangeable instruments of R & D policy. The first is essential for promoting R & D for advanced technologies, the latter may help to create a general innovative awareness. In the course of the build-up of policies of technology and innovation and their appropriate administration it was an achievement of policy makers to enrich their instrumentation by all sorts of direct and indirect measures. Now the time has come to discuss their effectiveness more rationally.

Government support for small and medium-sized enterprises

6. A major subject of our discussions in the Six Countries Programme has been government intervention to the benefit of small and medium-sized enterprises (SMEs). Three relevant seminars on this subject were 'Small and medium-sized manufacturing firms' (6CP: Rothwell/ Zegveld 1977), 'Trends in collective industrial research' (6CP: Rothwell 1980), 'New entrepreneurship and the smaller innovative firm' (6CP: Sweeney 1981). For the justification of SME-directed policies some studies claimed that SMEs provide far more innovation than larger ones, which receive far more public support. However, the numbers quoted in support of this view make no sense, because the quality of innovations cannot be quantified satisfactorily: instead of a competitive polarity, there is a symbiosis and a complementarity between large companies and SMEs as shown by the following examples:

— Large companies provide for most of the initial steps of the major or basic innovations, including their massive market penetration and diffusion. An example are solid state devices in micro- and opto-electronics.
— SMEs use them in order to feed their own innovations (e.g. incorporation in small computers and peripheral units and a great variety of other products, supply of services etc.).
— Much of the business of SMEs is supply to large companies. It is on the basis of the latter's specifications that many innovations take place in SMEs. This is consistent with the finding of ISI that most innovations of SMEs are triggered by demand from their customers (Meyer-Krahmer/ Gielow/Kuntze 1984).
— Spin-offs from large companies may be the seed for new innovative companies (e.g. in the chip and computer industry).
— Strong and growing small companies are being bought up by larger ones for strengthening their market potential.
— A network of SMEs up-stream and down-stream helps large companies to redistribute commercial risks (in particular in car and aircraft manufacturing etc.).

Depending on size classification, SMEs provide for 50 per cent of the employment. This fact alone as well as international competition may justify the support of their R & D. In fact, since the 1970s instruments to help SMEs have proliferated in all our countries (Braunling et al. 1982). The first ones were tax reliefs and grants as a function of company size, R & D expenses, the number of R & D personnel, the rate of increase of the latter, or extramural R & D expenses. The following steps have been taken more recently, in some countries:

— The administrative and intellectual barriers preventing SMEs from participating in government programmes of direct aid, originally tailor-made for larger or more sophisticated companies, have been lowered.
— Programmes are being designed to diffuse particular new technologies into SMEs, for instance new manufacturing and office techniques. In the Federal Republic, these programmes are categorised as indirect-specific aid; indirect, because of the quite liberal criteria of selection of supported companies so that their number is quite large (several hundred or more), specific, because the technical area of support is quite precisely defined.
— Subsidised networks of consultancy, information and documentation services are being established.
— Grants are being provided for a limited period of time to SMEs hiring young university graduates, with the intention of promoting technology transfer from science to industry.
— Venture capital is provided to new entrepreneurs, supplemented by grants and low-interest credits.
— Regionally, in innovation or founder centres, in 'technology factories' and science parks, low cost land, accommodation and infrastructure are offered for breeding new companies, preferably technology-based ones.
— More generally, more efforts at a regionalisation or decentralisation of innovation policies are being made (6CP: Benghozi/Matheu 1982).

7. ISI has been quite active in evaluating these policies so that we think we have some evidence for the following remarks:

— The proliferation of indirect aid is probably not very cost-effective. Only a fraction of the invested funds are being used for the targets set (Meyer-Krahmer et al. 1984). Recently, Edwin Mansfield (1984) has documented this conclusion also for the United States, Canada and Sweden. More precisely, my point is this: Together with other ministries of the federal and of the various state governments, our Federal Ministry for Research and Technology has been able to raise the annual budgets for research and technology of West Germany so that we compare favourably with those of the other leading industrial nations. However compared with the sum of all public subsidies for the economy, the R & D budget is quite small. Indirect aid for SMEs decreases it further for the benefit of quite general grants; thus the 'entropy' of our R & D budget grows and its information input decreases.

Another perspective is the following: by a logical division of labour between a ministry for research and technology on the one hand, and one for economic affairs on the other, the former would support the advance of best practice, whereas the latter may help to improve average practice by its diffusion. It is this differentiation of roles which has led to the creation of ministries for research and technology in various countries, quite often in the face of strong opposition. Now we observe a step back in the Federal Republic of Germany by the Ministry for Research and Technology imitating possible functions of the Federal Ministry for Economic Affairs.

— The high rate at which policy instruments for SMEs are being introduced and modified reduces their effectiveness. Managers of SMEs are too busy to be able to follow these almost annual policy changes. There is also quite a redundancy of instruments, for instance in the Federal Republic, where federal and state policies compete. As a consequence, subsidised consultancy services have to guide

their SME customers through this instrumental profusion.
— SME directed policies should aim at a systematic learning process involving SMEs, public R & D institutions, information services, consultants, etc. Such a learning process takes much time, say a decade or more, to become eventually more effective. Self-reinforcing mechanisms must be created by mixing public money with market elements. As consulting bodies for industry, fully financed public institutions of civil servants are not sufficiently flexible to cope with today's rate of innovation; but neither are exclusively freelance consultants.
— Most university institutes are not in a position to serve SMEs well (6CP: Stankiewicz 1984; Krupp 1983).

8. Recently several European countries started to subsidise the generation of new technology-oriented companies. In West Germany a generation rate of 300 per year is expected with an average employment of ten after three years, at maximum. The short-term effect on the economy is therefore small. The long-term effect may be substantial should a Polaroid, Nixdorf or Sony be among them, but the probability of this cannot be estimated. Therefore, the sceptical question remains as to the possible effects of special government intervention described above as compared to the very many factors on which the birth and growth of companies depend.

Furthermore, most structural change occurs within existing companies and therefore, the great expectations raised by our support of new companies will probably not be fulfilled. We cannot imitate the US situation which led to today's Route 128 and to Silicon Valley (SRI 1984) because European countries cannot afford massive military and space programmes and I hope they will not do so. Neither can we imitate the speculative climate of the US financial market, which owes its existence in part to the inadequate pension rights of US citizens. Japan is successful in the absence of these two factors, which obviously are neither necessary nor sufficient conditions for innovation. To a large extent the gamble for new technology-oriented companies is an inter-regional zero-sum game between investors of public money and so its cost-effectiveness should be investigated carefully. So far, however, the amount of aid to SMEs is quite small relative to the large programmes of direct aid and to subsidies to some sectors such as shipbuilding, steel, air-and space craft. Thus — quite apart from the individual merits of the particular programme — support of SMEs can be justified on the principle of equity alone. As a matter of fact, some of these measures have been taken not so much in response to specific needs articulated by SMEs themselves, but rather by government officials reacting to current political fashions. We have here much more a push of instruments of technology and innovation policy rather than a response to a well-assessed demand.

9. My conclusion is that *our present innovation policies should aim at their own rationalisation, and at the increase of their cost-effectiveness, rather than at their proliferation.*

Where are our policies today?

10. After the war, although officially our governments subscribed to non-intervention in industry, a network of policies developed which now encompasses a wide variety of elements such as direct and indirect aid, support of R & D infrastructure and institutions, etc. This development was paralleled by the terminological evolution from 'science policies' to 'science and technology policies'; more recently, the comprehensive term 'innovation policy' has gained ground — indeed one of our workshops in 1980 was entitled 'National Innovation Policies' (6CP: Stuart/Kuntze 1982). Thus *we have ended up in an international competition among quite systematic innovation policies.*

11. But has this enrichment and refinement of our respective innovation policies borne fruit? Are we better off through them? Where do we stand today? There are no comprehensive assessments available to answer these questions but today's economic and political situation, whether our policies have worked or not, may be characterised by the following facts and trends:

— After averaging over the periodic recessions and boom phases of Fig. 1, the growth rate of the German economy seems to be approaching a value between 1 and 2 per cent per year. This is close to the average of 1.6 per cent of the past 150 years and small compared to the growth rates during the post-war recovery. Even in Japan, average growth rates have been decreasing steadily in the past 30 years (Fig. 2). Of course, in the very long run, fast growth cannot continue forever.

— Slow growth, combined with large increases of labour productivity — and this may be a fruit of our innovation policies — has .led to increased unemployment with particular hardships imposed on aging and young people as well as on women.

FIGURE 2
Growth rates of GNP in the Federal Republic of Germany and in Japan; five year averages.

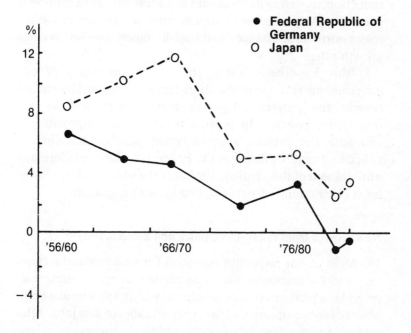

12. Since 1981, by a tour de force, France, for example, has tried to reverse this decennial trend by a series of measures which aimed at increasing the purchasing power of the people and by ambitious investment plans, especially in the big nationalised industries. This produced an incremental growth pulse of, at most, 1 per cent of the gross national product but at the cost of large public debts and foreign trade deficits. This policy is now being followed by a drastic austerity programme, so that neither a boom nor, still less, a lasting trend reversal has resulted.

The methods of the Reagan administration are different: the prescriptions are growth stimuli through public debts, massive armament expenditures, a reduction of taxes in favour of capital owners and cuts in social spending. By these means the periodic booms may become accelerated and reinforced, but no lasting reversal of trends can be expected, probably. Similar attempts by the Thatcher government also seem to have failed.

13. So, the long-term nature of the post-war trend of growth reduction, as well as its resistance to a great variety of economic counter policies, seems to suggest that we are undergoing a major structural change resulting in much smaller average growth rates.

If this hypothesis holds, the current measures of our governments reacting to the short-term business cycles cannot reverse the current long-term trend; much less so our innovation policies. In particular, it will be impossible to eliminate the present unemployment which, according to official estimates will last in the Federal Republic of Germany until the end of this century. Probably the situation is similar in most other countries participating in our programme.

New growth from micro-electronics and biotechnology?

14. Most of our respective ministers for research and technology and for economic affairs insinuate that micro-electronics provides a plethora of new products, which will stimulate new waves of consumption and hence, eventually, of new jobs. After several years of scientific and political discussion it has

emerged, however, that micro-electronics does not primarily create new, but rather substitutional, products which, compared to their predecessors, can be manufactured at higher labour productivities (Krupp 1980). Examples are electronic instead of mechanical machine-tool controls or electronic instead of electro-mechanical typewriters. But'the crucial point is that the electronically equipped manufacturing and office machines embody a considerable potential for rationalisation so that, on balance, the labour saving among the machine users far outweighs the jobs involved in their manufacture and in the sector of consumer electronics. Let us look at these arguments quantitatively.

— In the Federal Republic of Germany we have about 60,000 people making chips and other integrated solid-state (e.g. opto-electronic) devices.
— About 600,000 people incorporate them into equipment.
— Again ten times as many people, i.e. 6 million or more, will eventually use them in plants and offices.

Therefore, even if employment were to increase significantly in the first two subsets, it would be more than offset by productivitity increases in the third one.

This exponential rule shows that from the point of view of the whole economy and under our present circumstances, *micro-electronics does not produce a boom, but primarily a wave of rationalisation.* If the social consequences are redistributed evenly, this leads to a desirable reduction of work hours which ranges around one per cent per year and has been continuing for over a hundred years.

15. Looking further into the future, one may point to biotechnology. Today, genetic engineering processes are being developed for producing new chemicals, principally drugs, as well as new plant and animal species. Although this is of growing importance for our national economies, on the whole substantial economic effects will emerge only in a few decades. *In this century, a boom in employment and consumption based on biotechnology is not in sight.*

More growth by more exports?

16. Can exports be a major source of growth? Indeed, world trade has expanded considerably since the last war and exports have made sizeable contributions to our post-war boom. But the foreign trade of our countries is no longer growing at those post-war rates for several reasons.

The main importers of our goods are industrialised countries with the same phenomena of saturation and stagnation. In the case of non-durable consumer goods, no major increase in consumption is expected. As for durables, there is a transition to a merely substitutional demand. 'I cannot eat more than one cutlet per day and I already have a washing machine'. In household electronics some more up-to-date and supplementary trends are in sight, for example colour video machines and the compact disc, but the massive post-war period of first acquisitions has ended. Parallel to this, a change in attitudes seems to be gaining ground, at least in Europe: as the rate of growth of family incomes has decreased, the interest in new appliances has subsided. The car is being driven for a longer period of time; one no longer has to be among the first buyers of new goods. Certainly, these phenomena should not be overestimated; they may be partly reversed, e.g. through advertising, but they dampen the growth of consumption.

In the field of durable consumer goods the Japanese have been quite successful. Based on a very absorptive home market, they have developed excellent products and have built up very productive plants. But at the moment there are excess capacities worldwide which, as in the case of spun fibres, shipyards and steelworks, will have to be dismantled one day at considerable social cost.

17. By contrast, our volume of trade with the Third World is small, about 10 per cent. On top of this we are encountering increased economic competition from abroad, on two fronts: from the highly industrialised countries, above all the USA and Japan, as well as from threshold countries like South Korea, Taiwan, Hong Kong, Singapore, Argentina or Brazil. The

world market shares of the leading industrialised countries concentrate within quite a narrow margin as shown in Fig. 3., and *it is not probable that any individual country can step up export rates significantly without arousing protectionist counter measures* as experienced by Japan in the USA and Europe.

FIGURE 3
Shares of the world export market.

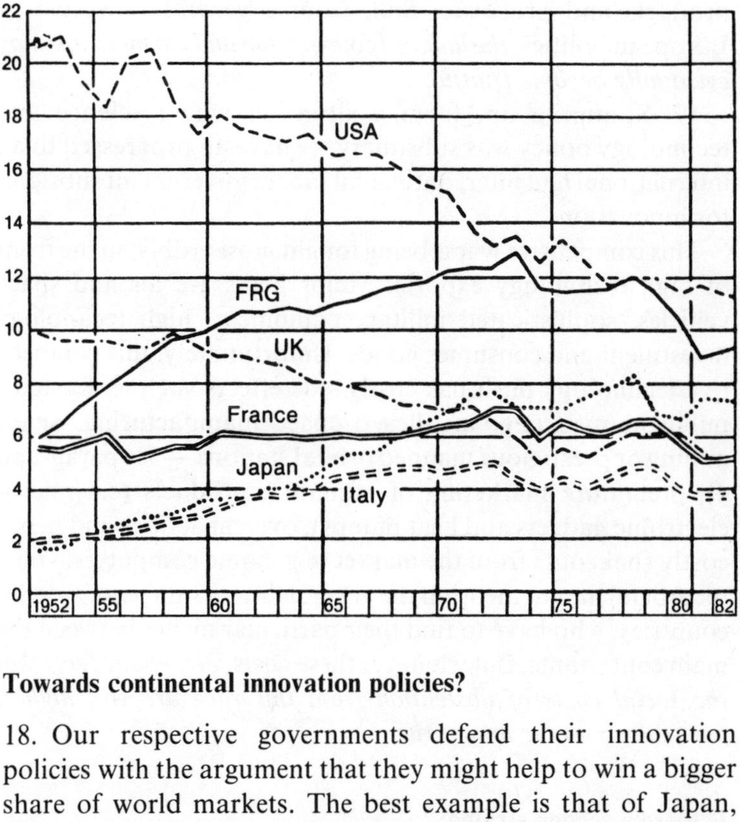

Towards continental innovation policies?

18. Our respective governments defend their innovation policies with the argument that they might help to win a bigger share of world markets. The best example is that of Japan, where in some sectors an integrated innovation policy of MITI in conjunction with well managed oligopolistic key companies has achieved outstanding success. This, in turn, has triggered the European Community to devise its *ESPRIT programme of direct aid to the electronics industry with a five-years' volume of 650 million ECU. It is argued that the companies and markets in*

Europe are so dispersed compared to those of the USA and Japan that concerted European action is required.

We may note in passing that, as mentioned in paragraph 4, the *cost-effectiveness* of this programme is *impaired by* the restriction of this aid to consortia of companies and to early stages of R & D. In such multilateral coordinations between companies and government agencies there is unlikely to be an efficient demand pull towards very specific competitive products and processes. Still, from a general viewpoint of European politics, *the induced cooperation and partnerships may eventually become fruitful.*

19. Summing up, from a situation where science and technology policy was subsidiary we have all progressed to an international and intercontinental race in government subsidies for innovation.

This competitive war is being fought most visibly on the front of high technology exports. Major items are air and space vehicles, sophisticated military equipment, high technology investment and consumer goods. Unfortunately, this competitive technology push has costly side effects such as waste of public money (e.g. in alleged space manufacturing, space mining or prestigious manned orbital stations — see paragraph 4), premature marketing of immature products (e.g micro-electronic gadgets and heat pumps), overcapactities and hence costly shakeouts from the market (e.g. home computers, video recorders); not to mention the general disadvantages of smaller countries, who have to find their particular niches between the main contestants. But whatever these costs, *everybody feels that the social costs of abstention from this race are still higher, particularly in the longer run.*

Is there a second strategy?

20. All *our national and European innovation policies are predominantly supply-oriented. They push new technologies,* they subsidise presumable industrial winners and SMEs, they diffuse new manufacturing and office technologies into our economy and promote rationalisation; and this in spite of dramatic

unemployment.

Let us ask, therefore, whether there is a second strategy. As we cannot escape the first strategy of supply push (see the preceding paragraph), the second strategy can only be a complementary one. For its identification, let us ask ourselves whether there is a manifest demand for such a second strategy. The subsequent paragraphs define this demand and attempt to elaborate a strategy for its satisfaction.

We live in a changed world

21. The years of our post-war boom were dominated by the general feeling of unlimited and cheap resources: energy, raw materials, water and environmental capacity for waste disposal. The multiplication of prices for energy and many raw materials as well as their large fluctuations and the poisoning of our environment with, as a result, more rigid environmental legislation, all point to fundamental changes in the supply of the essential factors of production to which the economy and politics will have to adapt. The first response of many economists to the pertinent theses of the Club of Rome was that technology would develop new and unlimited resources. Today, it is even more evident that this is quite improbable, at least at the costs of presently exploited resources. In spite of the fact that unlimited solar energy, for example, is available, it is generally more expensive than oil. The concentration of exploitable mineral resources is diminishing. Substitution and recycling are indeed possible, but only on a limited basis and often only at higher costs than those of primary raw materials. It is now beyond doubt that the capacity of the environment for waste disposal is limited. This is demonstrated even to sceptics by dying forests and fish, by the accumulation of poisons in the human body (e.g. chlorinated hydrocarbons, heavy metals), by widespread physiological reactions to air pollution (e.g. smog products), by pollution of ground water etc. etc. There are no technical, economic or political indications that suggest that this situation will ever be reversed.

This hypothesis of *a basic structural change* provides

indications as to new demand and therefore the kind and direction of desirable innovations and the investments required for their initiation.

Positive adaptation policies

22. A study by the OECD postulates 'positive adaptation policies' (OECD 1983). In our context this implies that *higher prices and scarcer natural resources require an increase in their productivity.* In other words, the input of resources per DM of produced goods and services must be decreased by means of improved or new processes, by substitution and by recycling. This applies to energy, raw materials, water and also to the waste disposal capacity of the environment. This process of increasing the productivity of our resources is under way: for instance, from 1970 to 1980 German industry increased its energy productivity by 20 per cent. Similarly, between 1973 and 1982 energy consumption in the European community decreased by 20 per cent (EEC 1984).

23. *The potential for increases in the productivity of energy,* on which I concentrate in these paragraphs, *will not be exhausted for a long time yet,* for three reasons:

— Firstly, the diffusion of the currently most economical processes is far from complete.
— Secondly, the number of sectors of the economy, in which the pertinent investments are economical, increases as a function of rising energy prices.
— Thirdly, the potential for energy saving is increasing owing to technical progress (e.g. improved control equipment, better heat resistant materials, increase of the efficiency of energy conversion).

An example of the third type, which also demonstrates that energy productivity and environmental protection tend to be correlated, are the wood pulp factories which, in the future, will be operated autonomously with respect to energy and almost autonomously with respect to water, by filtering the lignin out of the waste water and using it as a source of energy.

Alternatively, the lignin may be used as a raw material in the chemical industry. The purified waste water can be recycled into the production process. Another example is concerned with coal fired power stations, whose efficiency can be increased by a thermal coupling of the conventional processes with partial coal gasification. Thereby, fuel consumption and air pollution will be correspondingly reduced.

Outside of industry, too, there exists a considerable potential for energy saving. Improved architecture may reduce the heating requirements of new buildings by 15 to 30 per cent without active devices such as solar collectors or heat pumps. Reasonable heating and ventilation management and simple control devices in public buildings permit savings of energy of 20 per cent. The appropriate investments required to realise the potential of the first subset, viz. diffusion of the best practice, are cost-effective already at today's energy prices. This means that break-even between investments and energy saving may be achieved in three to five years.

It has been shown by ISI (Garnreiter et al. 1984) that economical capital investments by companies and individual consumers in order to increase energy productivity would reduce energy imports and create many new jobs. Quantitatively, the positive effect on the labour market would be quite substantial (see next paragraph).

24. While cost accounting of individual units of the economy can easily justify or stimulate a vast volume of investments for the increase of their resource productivity, this rationale fails in the case of environmental protection. The reason is that energy and raw materials are tradeable goods, which is generally not the case in the use of air, water and soil for the disposal of contaminants. Therefore, regulation is required for establishing environmental standards. Our growing awareness of the danger to the natural environment is leading to increasing expenditures for its protection — and recent attempts in the USA to reverse this tendency, or at least to slow it down, do not seem to have succeeded. Even though there may be a decrease in public awareness of some areas of pollution — the dying of forests will not be a long-lasting topic — new publicity will compensate in

others, for example in heavy metals in foodstuffs, pollution of drinking water and air, corrosion of buildings and materials, leaky garbage dumps, poisonous emissions in homes. Further, medical research will lead to a more accurate correlation between particular health hazards and particular pollutants so that public awareness will be kept awake and probably even increased, so that political action will continue.

The OECD has estimated (1981) that the annual cost to national economies of environmental pollution amounts to 3 to 5 per cent of gross national product. By contrast expenditure for the protection of the environment is at present only 2 per cent of the gross national product. For West Germany, a gradual doubling would mean additional annual investments of up to 40 million DM. Together with cost-effective investments for the increase in the productivity of energy and raw material resources these contributions could create 600,000 new jobs in Germany. This may constitute a major element of a second strategy for growth and employment.

25. How can this second strategy be financed? The increasing cost of resources is leading to a rise in costs for the consumer. However, in the medium term, higher investments to achieve a more rational use of energy can be more than offset by reduced energy costs; similarly with cost-effective investments for increasing the productivity of raw materials, including water, and for their recycling. In the long run, therefore, investments to increase the productivity of energy and other raw materials mean a reduction in costs for enterprises and consumers. A direct cost/benefit calculation for investments for the protection of the environment is not possible for an individual enterprise which emits pollutants. Pollutants cause costs outside the enterprise. But if an enterprise makes an investment to reduce the emission, the costs have to be internalised, usually by increasing the price of the product. In the final analysis, cost/benefit calculations must include the whole national economy, even that of other countries, since environmental pollution crosses national boundaries. High environmental investments by a particular country can mean increased burdens on its economy and short-term competitive disadvan-

tages for emission-intensive sectors of production. However, since all industrial countries find themselves in a comparable situation, their environmental expenditures will only differ to a small extent. This has been the case to date and will probably continue to be so.

26. Furthermore, investments to increase the productivity of resources produce innovations in goods and processes and thereby increase competitive strength. For the economy as a whole the proposed strategy of adaptation means that, in the short term, a small percentage of the purchasing power of private households would be used to decrease unemployment through the creation of jobs meeting the structural requirements and the strengthening of competition by innovations corresponding to the needs of future. In the long term, however, this strategy decreases costs for the national economy because of a higher productivity of resources.

Societal rigidities

27. For the execution of such policies for increasing the productivity of resources and for protecting our environment the OECD report already mentioned proposes measures to overcome 'socio-economic rigidities'. *It is not primarily the lack of new technologies which hinders this adaptation process, but barriers to institutional, organisational and legislative innovations.*

28. As a first example, let us take the field of energy. In the coming decades, in which the share of mineral oil in the supply of primary energy will decrease, the suppliers of electricity will have a key function, as their price policies influence the direction, the speed and the extent of the adaptation processes which consist not merely in increasing energy productivity but also in the diffusion of new energy sources. Economically the increase of productivity has, at comparable profitability, priority over the increase of supply, because it reduces fuel imports and relieves the environment.

The dilemma of the electrical utilities consists in the fact that they, like every other enterprise, want to maintain their usual business, if not increase it, and this on their traditional basis of sales of electricity from large power stations. In West Germany, the present regressive rates for electricity — in the European Community only Great Britain has similar ones — are basically not suited to encourage the rationalisation of energy use. Let us note in passing that Japan has progressive ratings which have stimulated important energy savings. The price policy, therefore, opens an important field of action. For industry, linear or even progressive rates for electricity would hit energy-intensive branches of industry, for instance in the sectors of aluminium, pulp and phosphoric acid. Thus our policy of open markets will be put to the test. But it has been shown by ISI (Garnreiter et al. 1982) that in most energy-intensive sectors of industry energy prices are not the principal determinants of their international competitiveness. Further, in the long run open markets and structural change of the international division of labour are beneficial to all countries involved.

The public electricity utilities also have a key role in the diffusion of small industry-owned power stations, heat/electricity co-generation, small running water power stations and, on a long-term basis, the production of photovoltaic electricity. It is being discussed in the USA as to whether one ought to leave the electricity utility companies in their key role, or separate the network and invite competitive feeding-in. A wise re-regulation of the utility companies would imply a new energy economy with a great potential for energy saving and protection of the environment.

29. To take another example: in West Germany about 20 per cent of primary energy is used for transportation. Energy saving would require that adequate public transport be offered to commuters. In large cities such as Hamburg, Frankfurt and Munich, appropriate incentives and disincentives are required to increase the use of public transport and to decrease public subsidies. By contrast, our regulatory situation comprises such contradictory elements as a tax on petrol, a reduction in the density of short distance transportation of the German Federal Railways and a tax reduction for commuters using their private cars.

In the medium term methanol probably ought to be used as an additive or substitute for petrol, thus reducing oil imports. For this, the taxation of fuel would have to change from taxation per unit of volume or weight to that of energy content. It may also be desirable to offset temporary decreases in oil and gas prices by increasing import duties, in order to stabilise the confusing price signals of the oil market, as is happening in Sweden, for example. In discussing the chronic deficit of the German Federal Railway its small environmental cost as compared to cars must be included in the cost accounting.

30. The costs of dumping waste and of recycling materials have to be integrated economically, in order to be able to offer recycled raw materials at more favourable prices. Similarly, an integration of sewage purification on the one hand and drinking water treatment on the other, as is the case in the Ruhr region, is more cost-effective.

31. The expected tightening of air pollution regulations will lead to increasing quantities of fly ash and gypsum from power plants burning fossil fuel. Instead of being dumped, the annual six million tons of ashes alone from the pit-coal plants in West Germany can cover a large percentage of the requirements of building material — as they already do in part. Arrangements will have to be made for intermediate storage — this material becomes available mainly in winter, while building construction tends to peak in the summer — for sales channels and for appropriate material testing standards.

32. The environmental policy of high smokestacks does not reduce emissions and creates, in individual cases, unsurmountable difficulties. Thus, a ceramics artisan in the Kannebecker Land in West Germany cannot afford a smokestack, quite apart from the fact that the amount of fluorine emitted is negligible compared with that of large emitters in the vicinity. Such cases have stimulated new regulatory concepts which are being tested in the USA — for instance the so-called bubble concept and that of saleable emission certificates. They attempt to introduce an economic rationale into environmental protection in order to make it more flexible with respect to sectoral, local and regional aspects. Because the issue is so

complex, the regulators and the executing authorities are faced with serious decision problems. Thus, transfer payments by communities to individual companies that are undesirable constitutionally, might be reasonable in the case where a discharger of cadmium waste would otherwise force the community to considerable expenditures for the cleaning of sewage sludge or its disposal. This would also promote the use of the sludge in agriculture, cutting down on fertiliser. Cadmium extraction at the polluting source is more cost-effective than in the sewage plant, where the cadmium is much more diluted.

As the example of the new asbestos substitutes demonstrates a strategic environmental protection policy triggers many innovations so that, for example, many uses of heavy metals, that still seem indispensable, may be abandoned. This could also be true for cadmium which is an ubiquitous pollutant.

Towards systemic innovations

33. The number of examples that may be be quoted is infinite. They all show that *'socio-economic rigidities' must be removed and those specific frame or context conditions created, within which market forces will lead to increased resource productivity.* Such frame conditions would reduce investment risks, encourage investors and stimulate those innovations and their diffusion, which fit with the direction of technical change, viz. those favouring adaptation to present and future prices and availabilities of resources essential to the economy and to society as a whole.

34. Supply-oriented policies for innovation can restrict themselves to promoting private enterprise which has developed very effective means to articulate and organise private demand and provide supplies to meet it. Here, decision making is quite simple; it generally takes place within individual hierarchically structured enterprises. The criteria are almost exclusively economic ones, modified by regulations designed to reduce all kinds of hazards concomitant with industrial activities. The exploitation of this quite simple feedback loop between

manufacturers and customers has led to an increase in living standards in the industrial countries, which is unique in history.

35. However, in the preceding paragraphs we have shown that our world has undergone major changes. Broadly speaking, it is in a state of transition from a world of rapid exploitation and waste of resources to one of higher resource productivity. Major areas affected are those of infrastructure and common goods where such simple feedback loops between supply and demand as described in paragraph 34 do not exist. Instead, *energy conversion and use, environmental protection, traffic, housing, renewal of cities, education, culture and other types of infrastructure and common goods occur in systems* characterised by the following features:

— Often the wishes of the customers are less concrete or are even conflicting (a mentality of safety, health protection and energy saving versus that of a 'sporty' car driver, especially in continental Europe).
— A consensus on standards for 'good' products or services as well as living and working conditions is missing.
— Decision making requires the coordination of a variety of institutions, often with conflicting interests (e.g. public utilities versus industry providing energy saving equipment).
— Decision rules are subject to a variety of criteria, other than purely economic ones (e.g. environmental protection).

It is this situation which causes what industry calls major uncertainties as to the future, which adversely influence their investment decisions, as well as employment and price policies, etc., thus impeding growth. The consequence of all this is that we need faster and more radical *innovation in the institutional and regulatory structures, into which technologies are embedded so that new and appropriate systems exert their demand pull on them. We need systemic innovations* (6CP: Tuininga, Fahrenkrog 1982).

36. More generally, by de- and re-regulation frame or context conditions have to be shaped in such a manner that the incentives provided by capital interests and profits are

reconciled with improvements in the quality of life of most people on our limited planet. Innovation is a rich potential and is not good *per se.* Context conditions have to provide for a selective environment favouring the more useful innovations, however difficult the criteria and the selective process may be.

We argue *the case for the organisation and articulation of new collective demand and its pull on innovation.* It is a policy which is hard to execute, certainly, because it requires interministerial decision-making and political manoeuvering in order to establish a path through divergent group interests. In Japan there is evidence to suggest that in this area of large markets of the future, it may again be Japan that gains the competitive edge on the other industrialised nations.

Conclusion

37. Let me conclude on a somewhat personal note: If we step back from our daily tasks and reflect for a moment, we find all of our countries embarked on one and the same competitive race. Our discussions of the competitive positions of our respective industries are centred on items such as video recorders, electronic games, home computers and faster cars as if our lives depended on them, whereas they actually do depend, literally, on measures such as environmental protection.

What people need are their own individual homes as well as high quality and useful consumer products manufactured by processes that minimise energy input, waste output and pollution. Furthermore, we want good infrastructure. Instead, a growing percentage of R & D is being directed towards armament and related products (e.g. space vehicles, fifth generation computers); in the USA it is already 70 per cent of the public R & D expenditures, and even in Japan it is growing. Our leisure time is being invaded by technologies whose usefulness, at least in some instances, is proportional to the rate of their non-use.

But economic interests and refined marketing techniques are stronger than the resistance of many people, insufficiently educated and tired by work at high productivity work stations.

This is symptomatic of the various deep inconsistencies of our precarious *conditio humana*.

Our Six Countries Programme has not contributed significantly to this discussion. We have generally only reacted to supply-side signals, with a lack of appreciation of 'true' demand, however vague this term may appear.

38. Technologies are embedded in society so deeply and in such a manner that innovation policies related to technology necessarily involve norms and values of the whole of society. Further, it is well known that technologies spread good and evil; they may be used most ambiguously. Some years ago technology assessment was promoted to analyse the interactions involved. *As a norm setter, however, technology assessment cannot succeed, because it* has to rely on subjective choices of variables, indicators, models, assumptions etc. and *typically ends up in political struggle between different interest groups.* Also, we must not expect our respective governments to support technology assessment liberally, as they have to be careful to please their electorate. Still, technology assessment may be a helpful tool to bring about a rational discussion of complex societal problems. However, also without technology assessment or ethical philosophy, appropriate innovation policies can be formulated and obvious evils be reduced. We are unpolitical and escape into our ivory towers if we shrink from discussions of norms. There is no 'science', such as technology assessment, to do it for us.

39. Technological advances will certainly be helpful in finding solutions to numerous future problems, but in some applications they may well make situations worse. What is required is a balanced approach to problem solving, using all available tools and innovation in all areas, i.e. social, economic, education, management and so on. Innovation in technology is only one area to be used in sympathetic cooperation with innovation in others. After all, a social innovation may serve the same aims and usually triggers the appropriate technological innovations (e.g. the ban on asbestos). It appears that, at least from a normative point of view, there is a great need for innovations outside the range of the usual technology policies.

An example is a reduction of the consumption of pharmaceuticals and a better percepton of the limitations of our health system by appropriate re-regulation and by educational measures. Another is new traffic regulations to reduce the toll of casualties on our roads. Therefore we have to ask ourselves: Can we reassess our societal priorities in order to innovate our innovation policies?

In the preceding paragraphs I have tried to indicate some major new goals.

40. And if we want to achieve a still deeper grasp of our situation, we have to go much further and ask such questions as: Can we continue to ignore the Third World as we have done in our Six Countries Programme so far? It is a key question because it points to the fact that *we live on a planet, which is limited in all respects and which will force us to solidarity one day soon, or else we shall not survive.*

These few remarks may remind us that, however well we may have done in our many seminars so far, we still have much further to go, if we want not only to serve particular sponsors, but to tackle the major problems which beset our societies and may eventually destroy them.

Uwe Kuntze helped me greatly with creative criticism and literature references. Mrs. Else Voyé showed inexhaustible patience with the many re-typings of the manuscript. I thank them both.

Literature

Achilladelis, B. et al. *A Study of Success and Failure in Industrial Innovation* (SAPPHO), Sussex 1971

Benghozi, P. J., Matheu, M. *Regional innovation policy: technology policies or regional policies.* Delft: Six Countries' Programme Report NO. 11, 1982

Braunling, G., Harmsen, D. M. *Die Wirksamkeit von Forderprinzipien und Instrumentarien der Forschungs- und Technologiepolitik.* Gottingen 1975

Braunling, G. et al. *Internationaler Vergleich der Forschungs-, Technologie- und Innovationspolitik fur kleine und mittlere Unternehmen in ausgewahlten Industrielandern.* Karlsruhe (ISI), 1982

EEC: *Comparison of energy saving programmes of the EEC member countries.* Brussels: Comm. (84) 36 final version, 1984

Garnreiter, F. et al. *Zur internationalen Wettbewerbsfahigkeit energieintensiver Industriezweige in der BRD* Karlsruhe (ISI) 1982

Garnreiter, F. et al. *Auswirkungen verstarkter Massnahmen zum rationellen Ener-gieeinsatz auf Umwelt, Beschaftigung und Einkommen,* Berlin 1984 (Umwelt-bundesamt Berichte 12/83)

Grupp, H., Schmalenstror, A. *Atome fur den Krieg. Ein Beitrag zum Zusammenhang der Atomenergienutzung und der Aufrustung.* Koln 1983

Keck, O. *Policy Making in a Nuclear Programme.* Lexington 1981

Krupp, H. *Technische Innovation und industrieller Strukturwandel,* VGB Kraftwerks-technik 62 (1982) 828-840

Krupp, H. *Den Wandel fordern.* Wirtschaftswoche 40 (1983) 134-141

Krupp, H. *Panel report on the functions of non-university research institutes in national R & D and innovation systems and the contributions of universities,* Technology in Society 5 (1983) 251-256

Krupp, H. *Zu den technischen, wirtschaftlichen und gesellschaftlichen Auswirkungen der Mikroelektronik, E und M Elektrotechnik und Maschinenbau* (Zeitschrift des osterreichischen Verbandes fur Elektrotechnik) 97 (1980) 75 — 85

Mansfield, E. *Public policy towards industrial innovation: An international study of direct tax incentives for R & D,* University of Pennsylvania, 1984. See also *Science 225* (1984) 700 — 701

Meyer-Krahmer, F., Gielow, G., Kuntze, U. *Wirkungsanalyse der Zuschusse fur Personal in Forschung und Entwicklung,* Karlsruhe (ISI) 1984

Nelson, R., Winter, S. 'In Search of a Useful Theory of Innovation,' *Research Policy* No. 1, 1977

Nelson, R. *Government support of technical progress: lessons from American history.* ISPS, Yale University, working paper no. 850, New Haven, 1982

OECD: *The costs and benefits of sulphur oxide control. A methodological study.* Paris 1981

OECD: *Positive adjustment policies: Managing structural change,* Paris 1983

Pavitt, K., Walker, W. *Government policies towards industrial innovation,* in Research Policy 5, 1976

Rothwell, R. *Trends in collective industrial research* Delft: Six Countries Programme, Report No. 8, 1980

Rothwell, R., Zegveld, W. *Small and medium-sized manufacturing firms: Their role and problems in innovation. Government policy in Europe, the USA, Canada, Japan and Israel,* Delft: Six Countries Programme, Report No. 4, 1977

SRI: *U.S. Government programs and their influence on Silicon Valley,* Menlo Park 1984

Stankiewicz, R. *University industry relations.* Delft: Six Countries' Programme, Report No. 13, 1984

Stuart, G. F., Kuntze, U. *National Innovation Policies: The challenges in looking ahead.* Delft: Six Countries Programme, Report No. 9, 1982

Sweeney, G.P. *New entrepreneurship and the smaller firm.* Dublin 1981 (there are also French and German editions available).

Tuininga, E. J., Fahrenkrog, G.A. *A systemic approach to innovation: Energy systems, energy conservation, recycling.* Delft: Six Countries' Programme, Report No. 12, 1982

CHAPTER 4

Innovation is entrepreneur-led

G. P. Sweeney

Entrepreneurship does not thrive in an environment dominated by large bureaucracies. Yet entrepreneurial investment in innovation – the entrepreneurial event rather than the innovation – is the source of prosperity and job creation. The creation of an environment in which the entrepreneur can thrive, is central to a systemic innovation policy. The market trends of the information age are providing the opportunity, but it is an opportunity which will require structural and institutional change if it is to be fully exploited.

After some years in local Government and the engineering industry Gerry Sweeney has since 1965 directed the development of the information services of the Institute for Industrial Research and Standards (IIRS), Dublin, of which he is currently an Assistant Chief Executive. He has written and lectured widely on the role of information and communication in innovation and industrial development and on the information economy. He is the present Chairman of the Six Countries Programme.

Introduction

'It is the dynamic competition among entrepreneurs, primarily in terms of industrial innovation, which forms the basis of economic development.'[1] In other words, the decisions which effectively determine macroeconomic growth are taken by entrepreneurs at the micro-level. The vitality of an economy and its flexibility to meet change are dependent on its entrepreneurial vitality, a vitality which finds its expression in the creation of new products and the founding of new firms.

The realisation of the central role of the entrepreneur has been a critical influence on the development of 'Six Countries' thinking and of the 'systemic approach'. The focus of this approach is that government policies and programmes to promote innovation as the main factor in economic growth should have support to the entrepreneur as their primary objective rather than support to research, industrial relocation, capital investment or other mechanisms.

Whatever the theoretical explanation for the current recession — the trough behind a fourth Kondratiev wave, another Schumpeterian cycle or other phenomenon — its major cause is a decline in investment in product innovation.

Behind this decline lies a dominance in most industrialised countries by large corporate bureaucracies not only of the manufacturing sector but also of the service sector — financial, distributive and governmental organisations.[2] The scale of this dominance appears to be greater than at any previous time in industrial history. Not only have the numbers of self-employed persons and small firms declined, but entrepreneurial vitality has declined. Whatever else their virtues, large mature bureaucracies are generally neither entrepreneurial nor innovative and are not, of themselves, creators of new wealth or new employment. Yet, historically, government policies to promote innovation and economic development have tended to be supportive of large firms. There are signs of change. Faced with rising numbers of unemployed, shed mainly by large firms, and by the heavy costs of supporting ailing industries, there is a growing awareness of the role of the smaller firm and of the founder of the new firm in economic vitality and growth. Where, for example, establishment of branch plants or relocation of large enterprises or establishments was seen as the means to provide growth in traditionally deprived or industrially declining regions, newer policies are focussed on self-generated growth through indigeneous entrepreneurial activity. This focus is expressed as support to SMEs — small and medium enterprises — demonstrating an apparent or assumed identification of entrepreneurial vitality with the smaller firm. SMEs have become fashionable. Few policy statements lack a reference to them.

Yet government itself cannot 'pick the winners'.[3] They are developed by culture and environment, by systemic policies not by bureaucratic analytical techniques or mechanistic policies. To develop such systemic policies there must be understanding of the entrepreneur, who he is, how he behaves and where he flourishes.

The entrepreneur

What then is an entrepreneur? Definitions are as abundant as the research literature on entrepreneurship. They have ranged from the innovator of Schumpeter[4] to the corporate managers of Chandler,[5] from the purely innovative to the purely routine,[6] to the extent that 'some authors wondered whether scholars should not discard the term entrepreneur on the grounds that so many different meanings have been assigned to the word that we are now confused.'[7] They illustrate that entrpreneurship is another segment of 'the human story in all its messy complexity' and provide a good reason why so many government policies fail or are neutral to development — the difficulty of grasping this complexity within a framework of legislative measures and public accountability.

Webster's dictionary grasps certain fundamentals in its definition — 'an organiser of an economic event, especially one who organises, owns, manages and assumes the risk of a business'. It does not however point to the vibrant humanity, which Keynes[8] described — 'Most, probably, of our decisions to do something positive the full consequences of which will be drawn out over many days to come can only be taken as a result of animal spirits — of a spontaneous urge to action rather than inaction'. Shackle[9] in discussing decision-making in the face of uncertainty, the essence of entrepreneurial action, described decision-making itself as 'the focal, creative, psychic event, where knowledge, thought, feeling and imagination are fused into action'. That it is psychic and made with feeling was confirmed by Keynes: 'Economic prosperity is excessively dependent on a political and social atmosphere which is congenial to the average businessman... we must have regard therefore to the nerves and hysteria and even the digestions and reactions to the weather of those upon whose spontaneous activity it largely depends'.

For Shapero[10], it is the entrepreneurial event which should be the centre of focus, and 'founding a new company is the clearest example of the entrepreneurial event.' It is this which provides 'a quality in economic life which is easy to recognise but hard to define, and harder still to place systematically in economic theory. Wherever development has most vitality, there seems to be an element of original adaptation, a restless adventurousness in the search for opportunity, which cannot be simply explained by the presence of exploitable resources. Let us call this quality entrepreneurship: a practical creativeness which combines resources and opportunities in new ways.'[11]

An entrepreneur then is someone who by a combination of knowledge, skills, creativity, imagination and intuition perceives an opportunity in the market for a new product or service and who, spurred by events and feelings, makes the decision to invest in this opportunity by founding a new firm and by organising this firm to survive and grow. Whether the opportunity is a technological innovation, a new use of existing technology, a creative design or a new way of satisfying user needs, the entry of the new firm creates change in the market. The entrepreneurial event is the dynamic of growth.

The role of the entrepreneur

The role of the entrepreneur in creating dynamic change is evidenced in prosperity, innovation and job-creation. The prosperity of a national or regional economy is related to the size of the small firm sector in that economy and to the buoyancy of this sector in terms of a high birth rate and as the seed bed of fast growth firms. Economies which showed the stronger growth up to the recession, Japan, France and Germany, had the stronger small firms sectors. Only Japan with much the largest small firm sector has seen continuing growth in the sector, from 70% of total industrial employment in 1977 to 73% in 1983.

The small firm sector which includes new firms starting small is a major source of innovation. 'Very frequently, innovations close to the market are carried out by small and medium-sized companies. Companies in these size categories are characterised by a particularly high degree of flexibility. This flexibility allows them to utilise quickly and at low cost new technical possibilities for conversion into marketable innovations.'[12] In the U.S., firms with less than 1,000 employees accounted for almost half of innovations in the period 1953 — 1973, and firms below 100 employees for one quarter.[13] Entrepreneurs are also more successful in long leap innovations.[14] Large firms whilst producing a majority of incremental innovations,[15] have a high dependency for major innovations on external inventors and small firms even for process innovations. Hamberg, Peck and Enos examining respectively the steel, aluminium and petroleum industries found this to be the case.[16] More recently, Mueller found that 102 of 226 process innovations in the food and manufacturing industries originated in small firms.[17]

Other studies such as those by Hamberg,[18] Langrish,[19] Mueller,[20] and the U.S. Commerce Technical Advisory Board,[21] confirmed the major role of the smaller firm as the innovator for the larger firm. As Prakke said,[22]

> 'According to a body of research dating back to the early sixties, small and especially new firms have made their own unique contribution to the technical innovativeness of many branches of industry and dynamic efficiency of the economy in general.'

Indeed, in terms of efficiency, firms of less than 1,000 employees produced 24 times as many major innovations per R & D dollar as large firms of over 10,000 employees.[23] In the U.K. 'results confirm the view of those economists who suggested that the innovative efficiency of small firms (less than 200 employees) may be greater than that of large firms, in the sense that they apparently produce more innovations per £ of R

& D than their large competitors.'[23] Gellman[24] found that small firms produced 2.5 times as many innovations as large firms relative to the number of people employed and did so in a shorter time.

The achievement of smaller firms in this regard is even more remarkable when one considers the increasing dominance of the large firm and the overall decline of the small firm sector in most developed countries. They occupy a smaller sector of the economy. Furthermore, entrepreneurial vitality and innovation should not be associated solely with high technology. In one estimate,[25] of the 16,000 new industrial firms founded annually in the Federal Republic of Germany, 800 can be regarded as innovative in the narrower and 3,500 in the wider sense, but all contribute to the economic vitality of the country. The real innovation is the founding of the new firm. Indeed it has been claimed that of the more than 20 million new jobs created in the U.S. since the beginning of the 1970s less than 3% were in high technology.

Entrepreneurial activity in small firms and new firms is the main source of new employment. In the U.S., Birch[26] claimed that small firms with 20 or fewer employees created 66% of all new jobs, those with less than 50 employees 87% of new jobs. In Japan, firms employing fewer than 30, representing 38% of total employment, accounted for 55% of employment growth.[27] In Canada, between 1971 and 1977, firms employing less than 20 represented 30% of total employment but created 59% of new employment.[28] In the U.S. electronics industry, as compared to mature firms, 20 years of age and older, start-up firms created 115 times the number of jobs, 5 to 10 year olds 55 times, 10 to 20 year olds 20 to 40 times.[29] Between 1970 and 1977, the Fortune 1000 largest industrial concerns owning over 80% of industrial assets increased employment by 3.9%, the rest of the private sector by 65% and government by 31.1%.[30] This relativity and the dominant role of the smaller firm has been confirmed in other studies.[31]

Characteristics of the entrepreneur

Instigating an entrepreneurial event by setting up a company is done by some people and not by others, and it is done in some places more than in others. It is a highly personal and individual event. Much research has been devoted to the psychology, the personal characteristics and the pressures which lead to the actual entrepreneurial event of setting up a new company.

Whilst need for achievement is a common characteristic of entrepreneurs, it is not a distinguishing characteristic. That which distinguishes the entrpreneur is the belief in their ability to control the outcome of their efforts, 'the belief in internal "locus-of-control"'.[32] Rotter's 'locus-of-control' theory states that an individual perceives the outcome of an event as being either within or beyond his personal control and understanding. 'If the person perceives that the event is contingent upon his own behaviour or his own relatively permanent characteristics, we have termed this a belief in internal control'. It has been demonstrated by Shapero,[33] Brockhaus[34] and others to be a common characteristic amongst successful as against unsuccessful entrepreneurs.

Culture appears to be a determining factor in developing internal 'locus-of-control' —culture in the sense of the environment in which the future entrepreneur has grown up or has developed into maturity, and including the following of role models. A majority of founders of small firms are the children of fathers or mothers who were themselves self-employed or owners of independent businesses or independent farmers, again a dominating characteristic.[33-35] Women entrepreneurs have fathers who were independent.[36] An entrepreneur who starts a company may stimulate employees to do the same and employees who do so encourage their colleagues to follow suit.[37-38] Where entrepreneurs originate in larger firms, they tend to follow the example of a colleague who has already succeeded in setting up independently, and new companies are much more likely to be founded by people who have worked in small firms or in small divisions of large firms.[37] The syndrome of following a role model, 'if he can do it, I can', seems to reinforce an already present internal 'locus-of-control' by making the action of setting up on one's own credible, but the culturally in-built 'locus-of-control' is dominant. Susbauer[39] found that entrepreneurs had either been told by their fathers never to start their own company or had fathers who were unsuccessful. There is a strong propensity for new firms to be founded in localities which have a high number of small firms and a large percentage of employment in them. Indeed, 'the larger the number and variety of entrepreneurs in a particular culture, the greater the probability that individuals in that culture will form companies'.[40]

Internal 'locus-of-control' may well be the reason why entrepreneurs are less conscious of the risk of their venture and therefore view the risk somewhat lower than the bankers and others whom they approach for assitance. Optimism of the economic climate or of the local environment may further dull the perception of risk and uncertainty. On the other hand, risk and uncertainty may act as exciting stimuli.[41]

Internal 'locus-of-control' seems to be reinforced by experience of entrepreneurship. Most failed entrepreneurs try again. New firms have a much greater chance of successful survival if founded by someone who has failed at least once if not twice in earlier ventures.[42-43] The earlier ventures have provided a learning process which enables the entrepreneur to reinforce his belief — there were factors of which he was previously unaware, now he can control them. The second business tends to have a product orientation, better initial financing and a balance of essential skills amongst employees.

The presence of internal 'locus-of-control' would however not appear to be sufficient of itself. 'Negative factors appear to be far more instrumental in precipitating entrepreneurial actions than are the positive factors that loom so large in the literature of rational approaches to starting a new company, such as perceived market opportunities'.[44] This is the displacement factor. Most entrepreneurs are pushed rather than pulled into action. Refugees are a main source of entrepreneurs. Unemployment, threat of transfer, even by promotion, to an undesired location, job dissatisfaction, even time of life, age, are displacement factors which push the nascent entrepreneur, the man or woman with internal 'locus-of-control' into action. Early death of a father or another event which threatened or disrupted the home and early life seem to be further forces which push the individual to control events. Frustration and boredom in employment, job dissatisfaction, are a powerful push. 'A noticeable percentage of technical companies are formed after a technical professional has proposed a particular product or service or project to an employer and has failed to find acceptance'.[45] Brockhaus found that the greatest dissatis-faction in previous employment of entrepreneurs was the work itself, not pay.[46] The emigration of frustrated men from corporations has been identified as a prime source of engineering companies in the U.K.[47] Successful entrepreneurs would seem to have had greater job satisfaction with previous employers than unsuccessful.[46] Determination never to be trapped is a powerful stimulant.

Emphasising the non-rational process of the entrepreneurial event is that a large proportion of entrepreneurs, including high technology entrepreneurs, had no idea formed or specific plan for the future at the time they left their previous employment or decided to start a business.[48,49] Indeed Shapero noted[50] that in his field research only one of the hundreds of entrepreneurs interviewed claimed to have planned a step by step process leading to the formation of their business.

Other entrepreneurs are not so much directly pushed as in a state of being between things —leaving the army or prison, completing a project, or the 'empty nest' syndrome of mothers. Yet others are pulled into founding a new company — a legacy, offer of a contract from a customer of their current employer or from their employer in the case of larger organisations. Sub-contracting is a major factor in the start-up of new engineering companies,[51] but one which has been declining in the face of increasing domination by large companies. The habit of integration, takeover of suppliers, in the West contrasts sharply with the Japanese corporations who rely much more on smaller sub-contractors both for efficiency in production and for innovation. This is undoubtedly a major factor in giving the

Japanese economy greater flexibility and vitality.

Sub-contracting as a start-up opportunity and as a mode of continuing business has declined also for other reasons — rationalisation and concentration of production especially after take-over, relocation outside of inner cities, spread of branch plants. Macrae's[52] apparently romantic view of Japanese entrepreneur out on the golf course hunting for new business whilst his secondhand robot bangs out components gives a pointer to the continuing vitality and competitiveness in the Japanese economy. The real pressure for robotisation/automation comes from small firms.[55] It allows the entrepreneur to devote himself to his real business of developing new markets, new products and managing the firm.

Sub-contracting to a former employer or to a customer of a former employer is one aspect of another major characteristic of entrepreneurs — the technical expertise of entrepreneurs, including high technology entrepreneurs, is strongly related to previous employment. The predominant majority, over 90%, have previous experience in the same industry[54,55] and 80% of new firms had products or services associated with the founder's previous technical experience.[54,56] New technology based firms (NTBFs) are usually founded by people who spin-off from larger corporations or other NTBFs.[54] Hence, the new business is founded around the technical expertise of the founder, and this is often a narrow expertise. Yet as the business develops the entrepreneur requires different mixes of skills. It is not surprising therefore that the better educated entrepreneurs have a better rate of survival and growth. Managerially experienced entrepreneurs generally show better growth, and their products are not so rooted in previous experience. Firms founded by a group of founders with a mix of skills also show better growth and survival. They have the range of managerial, marketing as well as technical skills to develop the business. As well as showing a higher rate of failure, 'craftsman' type of entrepreneurs have a technical or technological fix — their prime interest is in the technical product or production process problems.[57] Too much education is also a disadvantage. Those with PhDs have a tendency to focus on research or consultancy rather than products.[58] However, overall, entrepreneurs are better educated than the general population — although less so than managers in larger corporations.[59]

The firm set up by the entrepreneur is highly personalised. It must be maintained within his control. He devotes his life, his family, his material possessions to his venture. His and his family's equity overcome the cash flow problems. Control is in his own hands. As the company grows, new managerial staff may be taken on. These are his personal selection and team, control is still the entrepreneur's. If the firm is to grow larger, two things will happen. A much higher input of capital will be required and the financiers will want a bigger say, and a seat on the board in order to share in control. Growth will also lead to development of a corporate structure, staffed by professsional managers. The founder may still maintain a drive but eventually that entrepreneurial innovative capacity will fail —probably the reason why mature companies, that is companies which have passed their twentieth birthday more or less, are not major sources of either innovation or new jobs.

Many entrepreneurs therefore refuse further growth and stay at a point where they see themselves as in control. Their belief in their ability to control events has limits. However, information technology may provide a partial answer. Given the capability of micro- and mini-computers to process and present information, use of these may enable an entrepreneur to expand the span of his personal control. Whilst there appears to be no direct evidence of this expansion of control, there is evidence that small firms which use computerised management information systems have higher profitability and growth in employment than those which do not.[60]

The above set out three of the four major elements identified by Shapero[61] as going into the company formation process:

— an apparent disposition on the part of the nascent entrepreneur — the internal locus-of-control;
— the act of forming a company has been made credible by role models, either of parents or colleagues or is socially acceptable in the local culture;

— some displacement event precipitates the action by the nascent entrepreneur.

The fourth is:

— availability of resources which make the act of founding a company both economically and technically feasible.

This availability of resources includes the resources of the entrepreneur himself, his technical and managerial skills, and financial resources. But perhaps most of all it is dependent on information — to enhance skills, to provide new ideas and to provide the basis for decision-making.

The entrepreneur and information

Entrepreneur vitality is strongly related to information, its accumulation and its flow. It is the vital resource of the entrepreneur and the factor which nourishes his growth. It is complex because it covers every aspect of his business, and is dependent on the characteristics of the locality in which he sets up and on his own and others' personal characteristics. It can be divided into three kinds — stock of knowledge, nutrient and logistic information.

The stock of knowledge is that knowledge possessed by the entrepreneur and by the locality in which he sets up business. This stock of knowledge is made up of cultures, skills, and experience. Culture is an important element. It is partly the entrepreneurial culture of a locality — the examples of others, an already strong small firm sector, the tradition of being self-employed or setting up one's own business also partly the aesthetic faculty, the tradition of taste, skills, feel for the well made, well designed product. Whilst this aesthetic faculty may have a long historical tradition in traditional crafts, its continuing presence through technical change may be the critical factor in creative use of new materials and technology — as can be seen, for example, in the Italian furniture industry, where plastics materials are used not only with creative design flair but also with technical excellence. Skills embrace all levels of technology acquired through education and training in earlier years and experience since. The skills of the entrepreneur at start-up are usually narrow, but often excellent in his field. This latter point does not appear to have been researched *per se* but rather emerges from the literature. It is consistent with the need for achievement common both to entrepreneurs and managers.

The stock of knowledge possessed by the entrepreneur is the basis on which he sets up his business or has his original and later innovative ideas. For the business or the ideas to succeed he needs both nutrient and logistic information,[62] and both of these are strongly related to the stock of knowledge of the locality in which the entrepreneur, especially the technical entrepreneur, sets up business. The immediate channels of information, his networks, are local ones — his business and personal friends.

Nutrient information, as the term implies, is that information which nourishes the stock of knowledge and leads to creativity. It consists of attendance at conferences, courses and exhibitions, talk with suppliers, customers and fellow entrepreneurs, going on holiday, all the informal reading, meeting and talking of everyday life — and chance. Chance appeared in Shackle's list of information sources which started with Research, and the other norms of management information.[63] Browsing, finding 'it' in the book next to the book being sought, has been quoted by Shapero[64] as being consistently the source of 18% of innovative ideas. Browsing is the essence of nutrient information, the continuous receiving of awareness of new things and happenings through talk with friends and acquaintances in one's own local business and social networks and through random observing, listening, watching and reading.

Logistic information is that information which is required for decision-making in managing the business and for implementation of the idea. The question is known but not the content. It has been postulated that the cycle time between demand for the information, the identification of the problem and definition of the question, and the supply of the information is the determining factor in the efficiency and effectiveness of decision-making.[65] This cycle time between demand and delivery is therefore essential to the survival of an entrepreneurial venture as well as to any small firm, and it relates to internally generated as well as to externally generated information. Logistic information includes management information, the information required for the control and direction of the business. Most small firms fail for management rather than technical reasons. Their internal management information systems have been inadequate.

The desire to reduce the cycle time between demand and supply leads to large firms and bureaucracies congregating in localities where there is information-intensive contact. Information-intensive contact is a major reason for the growth of large urban agglomerations and this growth is intensified where there is a heavily centralised government, as for example in the U.K., France or Greece. 'Numerous communication studies have revealed both the high level of face-to-face contact maintained by senior office staff, and also that most contact sources are within half an hour's travelling time of one another. Indeed, Swedish researchers[66] have developed the notion of "contact potential" and have derived indexes to determine the business implications of communication and information variations between urban centres'.[67]

This information-intensive contact leads to centralisation of the headquarters of large corporations in large urban centres. They establish, in close proximity, their own information-intensive activities of research, marketing, financial control etc. and the effect becomes self-reinforcing. Service activities such as research and consultancy also locate in these same centres to be close to their dominant market. The large urban core region provides economies of scale in information access and acquisition. Whilst the primary reason for this geographic concentration might be to reduce the cycle time in receipt of logistic information, it results in intensification of nutrient information flows. It becomes easier to stay abreast of new developments in technology, design and markets. That is, the stock of knowledge is continuously nourished and the potential for creativity and innovation is optimised.

However, this potential for creativity and innovation is not necessarily fulfilled, whether by large organisations or by small firms. The nature of large bureaucracies inhibits entrepreneurial activity. 'The temptation to reject new concepts grows, rigidity sets in and change is resisted because it threatens the hierarchy of power and prestige on which the firm's system of control is built. The use of quantitative decision-making procedures limits a firm's ability to act on necessarily qualitative speculation about future markets and technologies'.[68] Localities which are dominated by large bureaucracies are not centres of entrepreneurial vitality, partly because there is a lack of openness in the flow of information from the large to the small. Large bureaucracies prefer to talk to large bureaucracies.

On the other hand localities with entrerpreneurial vitality are characterised by a richness and ease of information flow both between entrepreneurs and between entrepreneurs and the infrastructure of research, government, bankers and consultants.

Localisation of entrepreneurship

In fact, entrepreneurial vitality is very much a local phenomenon. It happens in some places and not in others and as a result economic development 'is a less than national phenomenon. It does not happen in general; it happens to specific people in specific places'.[69] Prosperity and economic growth of regions and localities are strongly associated with the strength and vitality of the small firm sector in the region or locality. 'The evidence supports the existence of a positive relationship between the rate of economic growth and the rate of new enterprise formation at the regional level — as it does at the national level.'[70] In the U.K., there is a good correlation between the level of income per head and the proportion of small establishments by region.[71] In the U.S., the regions with the highest rate of growth in new and small enterprises have the highest growth in income.[70] And regions with the lowest rate of foundation of new firms also have the lowest employment growth. There is similar evidence elsewhere in Tuscany with its high wage rates[72] and in France.[73]

Continuing vitality and prosperity appear to be dependent on the diversity within the small firm sector. Localities with a diversity of technology and industry have not only a higher vitality but a more continuing vitality.[74] 'Where variety and diversity abound, there is a higher likelihood for achieving meaningful associations of items not previously associated, one definition of creativity,'[69] as a comparative study of Manchester and Birmingham demonstrated.[75] In the nineteenth century Manchester appeared to be the paragon of industrial structure and infrastructure. Its core business of cotton manufacture was based on natural resources of ports and water, and led to the development of textiles engineering, chemicals, dyeing, printing and related service industries. In contrast, Birmingham showed a messy industrial structure. It had no specialisation and a lot of very small businesses, characteristics which gave Birmingham certain dynamic qualities', 'a capacity to create new work from their existing work'.

Areas which have a strong small industry sector continuously renew their vitality.[76] Founders of new small businesses tend not merely to have parents who were independent but to have worked previously in small businesses or small divisions of large firms.[77] Even in the U.S. with its high mobility, two thirds of new entrepreneurs set up in their own locality,[78] and they reinforce their own action by encouraging friends and colleagues to do likewise. Enriching of the vitality is further reinforced by the information flows. New entrepreneurs, particularly technical entrepreneurs, quickly form informal networks with other new entrepreneurs in the locality.[79] Before founding their business, new entrepreneurs have intensive informal contact with consultants in research centres, finance and other businesses. There are intensive and varied information flows in localities with high entrepreneurial activity, between suppliers, customers, entrepreneurs in other sectors and the same sector and with the service infrastructure. All these flows, contacts and bonds reinforce the entrepreneurial culture and strengthen the vitality and therefore prosperity of a locality.

The entrepreneurs themselves are major contributors. People with internal 'locus-of-control' more actively seek information and knowledge relevant to their situation,[80] they are better informed[81] and are more proficient in processing information.[82] As a result, entrepreneurship in the commitment to the entrepreneurial event seems to reflect superior information.[83]

The richness in information flow happens in some localities and not in others. It is indifferent to the actual information wealth of the infrastructure in univesities, research institutes, finance houses and consultancy and other information organisations. 'Cities and regions appear to vary markedly with respect to successful generation of new technologically based enterprises ... important factors exist which go beyond such indices as the total number of scientists or the total R & D expenditures or the availability of capital.'[84] Deutermann[85] investigated why two cities, Philadelphia and Boston, apparently with comparable infrastructure, exhibited such strong differences in entrepreneurial vitality. Shapero,[86] intrigued by the ubiquitous presence of venture capital firms in urban centres which were also endowed with universities, research institutes etc., but with different levels of entrepreneurial vitality, investigated the venture capital firms. Deutermann found a sympathetic responsiveness in the universities and banks of Boston which was absent in Philadelphia. Shapero 'inadvertently' found an openness to give information in the venture capital firms in the entrepreneurial cities, absent in the cities with low entrepreneurial vitality. Furthermore, 'technologically based firms in Philadelphia seemed to have less contact with suburban firms than their counterparts in Boston.'[87]

In other words, localities having high entrepreneurial vitality have characteristics similar to those of technically progressive firms, openness in giving as well as taking information, continuing effort in their own search for information and good internal communication flows.[88] The vitality, once initiated, becomes self-reinforcing and sustaining. The stock of knowledge of each unit is continuously exposed to new inputs from rich information flows, because there is a wide diversity in the information flowing. There is more immediate and responsive contact for information required for decision-making. An apparent independent self-support in information exchange is developed by the locality.

In contrast, areas dominated by large firms tend to have low entrepreneurial vitality. Such firms have internalised their information resources and networks through integration of their operational and manufacturing activities. Areas dominated by branch plants of large firms, also have low entrepreneurial vitality, their networks are with their distant parent company. Sub-contracting, an important source of start-up for new companies is minimised by the large integrated firm and even more by branch plants. An important means of developing local networks for technology and information transfer is thus lost.

Entrepreneurial start-up and failure

A locality with high entrepreneurial vitality has a high birth rate and a high death rate of small firms. These births and deaths give a locality flexibility in meeting economic, technical and market change, but because the firms are small their deaths do not have heavy impact on the locality. New firms in particular have a high death rate. Possibly, up to fifty per cent fail within the first five years. Overall, small firms can fail because of competitive pressures, technological obsolescence, lack of skilled labour, succession problems and managerial failure.

Competitive pressures where there is saturation of a market can lead to failure of more mature small firms, but they are an important cause of failure amongst newer firms. Domination of large firms in a market, particularly in distribution, can lead to failure even though the product may have the right characteristics of design and innovation to meet the needs of the market. The resources required to create the market demand to offset the dominance of the large distributor by either an alternative distribution system or by creating market pressure to persuade the big buyer to carry the product are not available to the smaller entrepreneur. Drucker[89] has emphasised this point, by illustrating the opposite. New entrepreneurs, albeit in the personal service sector, who have started relatively big with several outlets have been able to use greater advertising to create the demand for their service and achieved success.

In areas of advanced technology or design, a large number of entrepreneurs create a new market which can grow rapidly, but this rapid growth may, eventually, centre round a few leaders. Others fall by the wayside. The dominant cause of failure is, however, managerial. Most entrepreneurs base their product and therefore their company on their own technical skills. The focus of their attention is naturally on the technical detail of the product and on production. This is the strength of the business, it is on this that it will grow. Not enough of their attention is on marketing, developing the next product and especially internal administration. It is noticeable that those founders with managerial experience at start-up — ex-managers and second-time entrepreneurs — have a higher success rate. Comparisons have shown that companies which plan do better than those which do not, even though they do not follow the plans. Firms founded by three or four partners having a mix of skills, including marketing and financial, also perform better than those founded by one person.[90]

This lack of managerial non-technical skills tends to exacerbate the problems of start-up. Financing the firm through its first five years is difficult. Once it has achieved some market penetration and demonstrated the potential of its product in the market, obtaining finance for expansion is relatively easier. At start-up, the firm is faced with final development of its first product or service, setting up production, paying employees, generating first sales, building a distribution network, and generating the next product — all demand working capital before cash from sales begins to meet costs. Hence, the valley of death syndrome, the period when expenditures rapidly increase, sales are only slowly increasing and return on investment declines very rapidly.

At start-up therefore the entrepreneur typically tries to keep his initial costs low. He looks for cheap premises — his garage, back-garden shed or old premises in the city or town. This latter was a traditional and important part of the infrastructure for inner city firms, but inner city renewal, urban planning and factory legislation have been eliminating the run-down premises as a cheap source of start-up premises. Indeed, these factors appear to have had a significant impact on the decline of inner city small firm vitality.[91]

Secondhand equipment from sales programmes is another important source of cheap capital. Unfortunately, the practice of selling off in large lots to a large purchaser in a main centre often prevents a nearby small firm from buying the specific items to improve its efficiency and quality. Government aids and other financing institutions lay down conditions requiring purchase of new equipment, which even with subsidy would increase the cash flow problems of start-up. Shapero commented that the second time entrepreneur does not buy both a new car and a new truck as he did the first time — a secondhand, even a delapidated, truck serves both purposes. One can also speculate on the impact of the low level of robotisation in Europe as compared to Japan and the lower availability of secondhand equipment. The robot can free the entrepreneur from production routines and give him the time for the information and human capital activities of his firm.

Small firms, and more particularly new firms, are at a disadvantage in borrowing money. They do not require the very large loan with its lower interest rate. They do not have collateral equivalent to the finance optimally desirable at start-up, and they have neither the track record nor influence in the financial market. Social welfare, pension funds, personal savings, high personal tax have restricted the availability of funds for the smaller investment. They are controlled by large institutions which prefer the large investment, and there is evidence to show that new firms are now smaller at start-up than in the 19th century.[92] They are also restricted to sectors with low entry costs.

Hence the significance of the 'sweat equity' of the entrepreneur and his family in start-up. His wife does the books, his children clean and tidy and pack at weekends, he works one hundred hours a week, all to make up for the lack for working capital. Many do not even seek adequate working on capital, preferring 'sweat equity' to the restriction of their personal control of the enterprise, by having to give the bank a say in the business or a seat on the board.

There is also the problem of fashion. High technology firms do offer greater opportunity than lower technology firms for rapid capital growth. They are also a fashionable investment. A recent OECD report[93] illustrates the predominance in 1982 of high technology — 68% of investment went to electronics related industries, computing, telecommunications etc. In Boston, there is a buoyant venture capital market for high-technology, yet Massachussets is industrially declining. The two may not be unassociated, given the more general evidence on the relationship between the vitality of the small firm sector and the sympathetic responsiveness of the infrastructure.

Venture capital availability for small firms has been the focus of much attention in the U.S. and Europe. In practice venture capital is mainly sought and obtained for expansion. The firm has survived the initial 'valley of death', it now wants growth. Capital for growth for lower technology firms is probably much more difficult. Governments are seeking by various measures to encourage venture capitalists to extend their range and risk in investment. These have been welcome but may have little influence. When asked, venture capitalists deny the influence of government aid schemes as a factor in investment making.[94]

The problems of start-up capital, particularly working capital, and the weak position of the new entrepreneur in getting access to it are drawing attention in the U.S. to pre-venture capital as the real problem area: provision of capital to carry out pre-production activities in final design, setting up production, training workers, carrying out initial sales, setting up distribution. These are the activities which impose a heavy drain in the early months of start-up and prevent the gaining of the potential market share sufficiently quickly to survive.

The number of companies which in fact receive support from venture capitalists or other institutions at start-up is small. 'New ventures almost never receive financial support from formal financial institutions'.[95] On the other hand, 'the presence of a financial community that responds positively to new companies is a key factor in whether or not a region will generate, develop, and keep new enterprises.'

Financing of start-up is often done on the basis of an advance payment from a customer — a source found to be significant in Sweden, where larger firms in effect sponsored the development of new companies. An immediate contract from a customer of the existing employer or from the employing organisaion itself can ease start-up. A particularly successful mode of financing a new manufacturing business is to set up first as an agent or distributor and provide cash-flow for manufacturing start-up from the profits of this low-investment quick-return business.

In summary, management skills and financing are the two dominant problems in achieving start-up and survival through the 'valley of death', but financing is the more critical problem in an age of high taxation and of concentration of finance in large bureaucratic institutions.

A future for the entrepreneur

Investment to support the entrepreneur and small firm vitality has the potential to be much more productive than other forms of investment in economic development or job creation. On the other hand the barriers to growth in the numbers of small firms and of new entrepreneurs are formidable. Industrial society achieved productive growth through economies of scale, mass-production technology and scientific management organisation. Undoubtedly, great wealth has been created, standards of living have been raised, education is more widespread but as the means of production, distribution, finance and government administration have become more concentrated in large centralised bureaucracies the system has been increasingly unable to provide flexibility, renewal and growth.

At the centre of this development has been the focus on price as the main element in competition and the growth of professional management. Price competition inevitably led to standardisation, rationalisation of products and production. Pressure on costs led to trade-off against quality, and to vertical integration and oligopolistic if not monopolistic control of large segments of markets. Professional management became necessary to coordinate and control the large and complex organisations which evolved. Risk was eschewed and takeover became a major means of growth. The result has been that small firms have declined in numbers, new entrepreneurs have greater difficulty in entering markets and are restricted to markets with low costs of entry.

There are however signs of change which may be best summarised as the evolution from the industrial to the information economy. Markets are becoming more fragmented and discerning. Higher standards of living give the ability to choose. Increased standards have created a new level not only of awareness but of taste. The consumer, private and corporate, increasingly wants products suited to his individual needs. He is demanding more creativity, more diversity, and better performance and quality in his purchase.[96] 'Design is tending to become one of the vital factors in innovation.'[97] Price is no longer a dominant factor, as has been demonstrated in the buying of tractors by British farmers.[98] 'Entrepreneurial activity is not focussed on competing on the basis of price.'[99] Communications, transport and the higher added value of an information-intensive product diminish the need to be close to dominant centres. 'Its main competitive advantage is not proximity to a richer expanding market but its ability to respond to international threats and opportunities emerging from changing tastes, technology, relative prices and competition.'[99]

The significant factor in the market change is that the knowledge, information and skills incorporated in the end product, its information-intensive component, will increasingly determine competitiveness. This component embraces design, technological excellence, performance in use, and close matching to user needs. 'Industrial creation has to reconcile technical, economic and aesthetic needs.[100] The users themselves are more information intensive. They are more aware and demand more information to increase their awareness. They seek value for money and therefore more information on which to base their choice. 'The trend towards the mature customer suggests a shift from image oriented adverts toward information oriented adverts. With the aid of more information, and the maturity to make use of it, consumers will shop with greater self assurance. This greater self-assurance will accelerate the concern for quality, demands for reliability and good customer service.[101]

Consumers are reacting against a production oriented manufacturing system and seeking a manufacturing system oriented to servicing their needs.[102] Servicing these needs involves a process of virtually continuous innovation and creativity and production of diverse and more customised products. Large centralised bureaucratic organisations are not suited to meet these needs. Flexibility, rapid response to change, diversity in production, creativity, require smaller units of organisation within existing organisations and in the industrial and service structure as a whole.

'In the era of human capital, an era that all industrialised countries are entering, high volume standardised production will to a great extent be replaced by flexible system production, in which integrated teams of workers identify and solve problems. This new organisation of work necessarily will be more collaborative, participating and egalitarian than is high volume standardised production, for the simple reason that initiative, responsibility and discretion must be so much more widely exercised within it. Since its success depends on quickly identifying and responding to opportunities in its rapidly changing environment, the flexible enterprise cannot afford rigidly hierarchical chains of command.'[103]

The entrepreneurial organisation of the information economy would therefore seem to be one structured at the level of the small unit of organisation, a small unit in itself or a large organisation broken down into such small units. Japan appears to be leading this trend. Qualilty Circles were a first step in this direction — the Japanese name for them being 'small group activities'. Kyoto Ceramic has broken into small virtually autonomous units integrating all functions within their product specialisation. Toyota sees itself breaking into smaller units each with a high level of information activities to produce customised vehicles. The trend is observable elsewhere. In the U.S., innovative firms are those with smaller more independent divisions and looser hierarchical control.[104] Firms in Italy producing information technology and at the forefront in internal diffusion and use of the technology, are demonstrating 'centrifugal force' at work,[105] decentralising into smaller units, each with autonomy in decision-making and integrating their research, design, and marketing functions. This decentralisation is being reinforced by the desire for a higher quality life-style and work style. 'The widening of both personal choice and life-style choices will be among the many big growth small scale industries, on sub-contracting to which larger firms will increasingly rely.'[106]

A further impact of these changes is that 'barriers to entry to a market by new small firms are diminished and the larger company anxious to retain market share and leadership relies for much of its input and indeed product range on buying from smaller specialised companies which are leading in specific areas.'[107]

Present indicators are therefore that the information economy will be a 'molecular' economy composed of small units of production and service, each being information intensive in its internal functions and organised around these but also being heavily dependent on and inter-connected with external information and networks. Information technology will be the nervous system of this economy, accelerating the trend to decentralisation, and supporting the increasing dependence on external information, and also providing a production system which is not only flexible in meeting changing needs but capable of efficient production of small batches.

It must however be said that there is another view of the information economy, that expressed by one of its leading analysts: 'An information economy is largely bureaucratic in nature; decisions are made and power is wielded not by many independent firms competing for a market but by relatively insulated private and public bureaucracies.'[108] And information technology could be used to reinforce the centralised bureaucratic structures and their dominance of economies.

Nevertheless, change seems inevitable given the changes in markets. The impact of these changes on the large bureaucratic structures will be only slowly absorbed given the nature of bureaucracies. The real question is whether these changes will have impact on renewed economic vitality by creating opportunities for a renewal of entrepreneurial vitality.

The role of Government

In most developed and developing countries government has a dominant influence. It is the largest employer, dispenses the largest funds, and in its hands primarily lies the creation of the environment in which entrepreneurship can flourish. There is now the additional factor of the emergence of the information economy which is driving government into a new role, a role not of service but of producer of raw materials.[109]

Economic growth is entrepreneur-led. Only the entrepreneur has the perception of an opportunity to enter a market or create a new market. The success of the investments in these is increasingly dependent on the information component of the end-product. The decisions of the entrepreneur are not only the real decisions which create economic wealth, they are the decisions which convert information and knowledge into economic wealth.

Government, analysis of the information economy reveals, is the main provider of information and knowledge, that is the main provider of what are now the main capital inputs into entrepreneurial and innovative development. Its role has changed. It has become an active rather than a passive service and the quality and timeliness of its provision of these capital inputs will be a major factor in the ability of an economy to respond creatively to technical change and market opportunity.

The information and knowledge inputs of government take place at three interdependent levels:

— the creation and maintenance of the stock of knowledge and its components of culture, skills and expertise, through

education, training and research;
— the stimulation of nutrient information flows, an awareness of what is happening at home and abroad, in research, technology, and markets, and the provision of the means for creating this awareness;
— the provision of logistical information, shortening the cycle time between the need for information and its supply.

However, entrepreneurial vitality happens only in specific localities or regions where there is diversity and quality in the information flows, responsiveness in meeting the needs of entrepreneurs, and openness in provision of information and where there is involvement in the local informal networks. For government inputs to have the effect of stimulating entrepreneurial vitality, the mode of operation of government activities must adopt new characteristics and structures. Government should lead structural change:

— decentralisation of decision-making to make it more timely and relevant to needs;
— responsiveness and openness in provision of information and services, to create an information rich environment;
— localisation of the interface, on a person-to-person basis, inter-linking the local informal networks to the local, regional and national formal networks.

In effect, the government structure should also be a molecular one, matching the molecular clusters of small units of productive economic organisation in such a way as to create a culture which will nourish entrepreneurial vitality and creativity.

The creation of such a culture is one of the elements of the systemic approach to innovation policy developed in the Six Countries Programme. In effect it is the creation of an environment which is information rich by re-uniting culture and technology into a single and pervasive technical culture. It is the combining of:

— the aesthetic faculty which governs (or appreciates) the quality of design of a product, its interface with the user,

matching his tastes and needs, and its diverse or unique character;
— the traditional crafts and skills which distinguish one nation or region from another but which on the one hand ensure the final quality of the product and on the other provide for creative diversity;
— the new technologies and pervasive technologies which are bringing new opportunities in themselves and are enriching innovation in more traditional sectors.

Perhaps the last word should be given to the Vice-President of Philips who, explaining the purchase of a share in Grundig said: 'and don't forget that the company is based in a part of Germany where mechanical arts and skills have been important for centuries.'[110] Culture is an inescapable factor in entrepreneurial and creative activity.

1. Freeman, C. et al, (1982)
2. Sweeney, G. P. (1984)
3. Nelson, R. R. and Langlois, R. N. (1983)
4. Schumpeter, J. (1934)
5. Chandler, A. D. (1979)
6. Sawyer, J. E. (1958)
7. Livesay, H. C. (1982)
8. Keynes, J. M. (1936)
9. Shackle, G. L. S. (1962)
10. Shapero, A. A. (1980)
11. Marris, P. and Somerset, A. (1971)
12. Niederwemmer, U. (1980)
13. National Science Foundation (1978)
14. Krasner, O. J. (1982)
15. Marquis, D. G. and Myers, S. (1969)
16. Office of Federal Procurement Policy (1977)
17. Mueller, F. W. (1962)
18. Hamberg, D. (1936)
19. Langrish, J. (1972)
20. Mueller, W. F. (1962)
21. Commerce Technical Advisory Board (1967)
22. Prakke, F. (1980)
23. Freeman, C. (1971)
24. Gellman Res. Assocs. (1982)
25. Nierderwemmer, U. (1980)
26. Birch, D. L. (1981)
27. Sweeney, G. P. (1981)
28. Bulloch, J. F. (1979)

29. Zschau, E. V. W. (1978)
30. NFIP (1979)
31. e.g. Commerce Technical Advisory Board (1978)
32. Rotter, J. B. (1966)
33. Shapero, A. A. (1975)
34. Brockhaus, R. H. (1980a)
35. Collins, O. F. and Moore, D. G. (1970)
36. Hirsch, R. D. and O'Brien, M. (1982)
37. Cooper, A. C. (1971)
38. Shapero, A. A. (1971)
39. Susbauer, J. C. (1972)
40. Shapero, A. A. and Sokol, L. (1982)
41. Gasse, Y. (1982)
42. Cooper, A. C. (1971)
43. Lamont, L. M. (1972)
44. Shapero, A. A. (1977)
45. Shapero, A. A. and Sokol, L. (1982)
46. Brockhaus, R. H. (1980)
47. Boswell, J. (1972)
48. Cooper, A. C. (1973)
49. Brockhaus, R. H. (1980a)
50. Shapero, A. A. (1971)
51. Economists Advisory Group Ltd. (1978)
52. Macrae, N. (1982)
53. Japan Robot Development Association
54. Cooper, A. C. (1973)
55. Susbauer, J. C. (1972)
56. Lamont, L. M. (1972a)
57. Smith, N. R. (1967)
58. Roberts, E. (1983)
59. Brockhaus, R. H. (1982)
60. McDonald, S. and others (1980)
61. Shapero, A. A. (1977)
62. Shapero, A. A. (1984)
63. Lamberton, D. McL. (1972)
64. Shapero, A. A. (1973)
65. Kendrick, J. G. (1983)
66. Tornquist, G. (1970)
67. Mandeville, T. (1983)
68. Lewis, J. D. (1982)
69. Shapero, A. A. (1977)
70. EAG (1978)
71. Gudgin, G. (1978)
72. Macrae, N. (1982)
73. Aubert, J. (1979)
74. Shapero, A. A. and Sokol, L. (1982)
75. Jacobs, J. (1969)
76. Shapero, A. A. (1972)

77. Cooper, A. C. (1973)
78. Boswell, J. (1973)
79. Cooper, A. C. (1971a)
80. Valecha, G. K. (1972)
81. Wolk, S. and Ducelte, J. (1974)
82. Dean, B. V. (1983)
83. Seeman, M. and Evans, J. W. (1962)
84. Commerce Technical Advisory Board (1967)
85. Deutermann, E. P. (1966)
86. Shapero, A. A. (1983)
87. Freeman, A. E. (1983)
88. Sweeney, G. P. (1980)
89. Drucker, P. F. (1984)
90. Roberts, E. B. (1983)
91. EAG (1978)
92. Dahmen, E. (1970)
93. OECD (1984)
94. Shapero, A. A. (private communication)
95. Shapero, A. A. (1977)
96. Department of Trade (1983)
97. Piattier, A. (1981)
98. Rothwell, R. (1983)
99. Pavitt, K. (1979)
100. Lang, J. (1983)
101. Ogilvy, J.A. (1984)
102. Sweeney, G. P. (1981)
103. Reich, R. B. (1983)
104. Peters, T. J. and Waterman, R. H. (1982)
105. Lamborghini, B. and Antonelli, C. (1979)
106. Macrae, N. (1976)
107. Sweeney, G. P. (1981)
108. Porat, M. U. (1978)
109. Sweeney, G. P. (1984)
110. Fox, B. (1982)

References

Aubert, J. *and* Laplume, Y. Innovation in the provinces: how does it happen? Seminar on the management of innovation in small firms. Tech. Inst. Jutland and OECD, 1979.

Bannon, M. J. Service type employment and regional development. NESC Report No. 28. Dublin, 1977.

Birch, D. L. The job-generation process. Cambridge, MIT, 1979.

Boswell, J. The rise and fall of small firms. London, Allen & Unwin, 1972.

Brockhaus, R. H. The effect of job dissatisfaction on the decision to start a business. Journal of Business Management, 1980.

Brockhaus, R.H. Psychological and environmental factors which distinguish the successful from the unsuccessful entrepreneur: a longitudinal study. Academy of Management Meeting, 1980a.

Brockhaus, R. H. The psychology of the entrepreneur. In Kent, C. A. et al. eds. The encyclopaedia of entrepreneurship. New Jersey, Prentice Hall, 1982.

Bulloch, J. F. The vital role of small scale enterprises in job creation and business development. 6th International Symposium on Small Business, Berlin 1979.

Chandler, A. D. Visible hand. Harvard University, 1979.

Collins, O. F. and Moore, D. G. The organisational makers: a behavioural study of independent entrepreneurs. Meredith, 1970.

Commerce Technical Advisory Board. The role of the new technical enterprises in the U.S. economy. Washington, Department of Commerce, 1978.

Commerce Technical Advisory Board. Technological innovation: its environment and management. Washington, Department of Commerce, 1967.

Cooper, A. C. The founding of technologically based firms. Milwaukee, Center for Venture Management, 1971a.

Cooper, A. C. Spin-offs and technical entrepreneurship. IEEE Trans. Engineering Management. EM 18(1) Feb. 1971.

Cooper, A. C. Technical entrepreneurship: what do we know? Research and Development Management, 3 Feb. 1973.

Dahmen, E. Entrepreneurial activity and the development of Swedish industry. Irwin, 1970.

Dean, B. V. A network method in the management of innovative start-ups. *In* Hornaday, J. L. *et al.* Frontiers in entrepreneurship research, 1983. Wellesley, Mass., Babson College, 1983.

Department of Trade, U.K. Standards, quality and international competitiveness. London, HMSO, 1982 (Cmnd 8621)

Deutermann, E. P. Seeking science based industry. Federal Reserve Bank of Philadelphia Business Review, May 1966, 3 —10.

Drucker, P. F. Our entrepreneurial economy. Harvard Business Review, Jan. - Feb. 1984, 59 — 64.

Economists Advisory Group. Small firms in cities: a review of recent research. Shell U.K. Ltd., 1978.

Fox, B. Has European industry a future? New Scientist, 7 Jan. 1982, 16 — 18.

Freedman, A. E. New technology based firms: critical location factors. In Hornaday, J. L. *et al.* Frontiers in entrepreneurship research. Wellesley, Mass., Babson College, 1983.

Freeman, C. The role of small firms in innovation in the U.K. since 1945. London, HMSO, 1971.

Freeman, C., Clark, J. *and* Soete, L. Unemployment and technical innovation. Pinter, 1982.

Gasse, Y. Elaborations on the psychology of the entrepreneur. In Kent, C. A. *and* others (1982).

Gellman Research Associates. The relationship between industrial concentration, firm size and technological innovation. Jenkinstown, Pa. 1982.

Gudgin, G. Industrial location processes and regional employment growth. Saxon House, Farnborough, 1978.

Hamberg, D. Research and development. New York, Random House, 1966.

Hirsch, R. D. and O'Brien, M. The woman entrepreneur as a reflection of the type of business. *In* Vesper, K. H. ed. Frontiers of entrepreneurship research, 1982. Babson College, Mass. 1982.

Jacobs, J. The economies of cities. New York. Random House, 1969.

Japan Robot Development Assoc. Private communication.

Kendrick, J. G. Cycle times of information. The Information Society, 2(2) 1983, 97 — 106.

Keynes, J. M. The general theory of employment, interest and money. Harcourt Brace, 1936.

Krasner, O. J. The role of entrepreneurs in innovation. *In* Kent, A. C. *et al.* Encyclopaedia of entrepreneurship. New Jersey, Prentice Hall, 1982.

Lamberton, D. McL. Information and profit. *In* Uncertainty and expectations in economics: essays in honour of G. L. S. Shackle. Oxford, Blackwell, 1972.

Lamborghini, B. *and* Antonelli, C. The impact of electronics on industrial structures and firms' strategies. OECD Special session on impact of microelectronics on productivity and employment. Nov. 1979.

Lamont, L. M. The role of marketing in technical entrepreneurship. *In* Cooper, A. C. *and* Komives, J. L. *eds.* Technical entrepreneurship: a symposium. Milwaukee, Center for Venture Management, 1972.

Lamont, L. M. What entrepreneurs learn from experience. Journal of Small Business Management. July 1972.

Lang, J. Minister of creation. Design, Nov. 1983, 58 — 59.

Langrish, J. *et al.* Wealth from knowledge. London, MacMillan, 1972.

Lewis, J. D. Technology, enterprise and American economic growth. Science, 215, 5 March 1982, 1204 — 1211.

Livesay, H. C. Entrepreneurial history. *In* Kent, C. A. *et al.* Encyclopaedia of entrepreneurship. Prentice Hall, 1982.

McClelland, D. The achieving society. Van Nostrand, 1961.

MacDonald, S., Manderville, T. *and* Lamberton, D. Computers in small business in Australia. Department of Economics and Institute of Industrial Economics. Discussion Paper No. 14. University of Newcastle, Australia, 1980.

Macrae, N. The coming entrepreneurial revolution: a survey. The Economist, 25 Dec. 1976, 41 — 65.

Macrae, N. Intrapreneurial now. The Economist. 17 April 1982, 47 — 52.

Mandeville, T. The spatial effects of information technology. Futures, Feb. 1983, 65 — 72.

Marquis, D. G. *and* Myers, S. Successful industrial innovations. Washington, Supt. of Documents, 1969.

Marris, P. *and* Somerset, A. African businessmen: a study of entrepreneurship and development in Kenya. Routledge, Kegan Paul, 1971.

Mueller, F. W. The origin of the basic inventions underlying Du Pont's major product and process innovations 1920 to 1950. *In* Nelson, R. R. *ed.* The rate and direction of inventive activity. Princeton, National Bureau of Economic Research, 1962.

Mueller, W. F., Culbertson, J., *and* Peckham, B. Market structure and technological performance in the food and manufacturing industries. University of Wisconsin, Madison, 1982.

National Science Foundation. Science indicators 1976. Washington, NSF, 1978.

Nelson, R. R. *and* Langlois, R. N. Industrial innovation policy: lessons from American history. Science, 219, 18 Feb. 1983. 814 — 818.

NFIP (National Federation of Indepdendent Businesses.) Fact Sheet. San Mateo, Ca., 1979.

Niederwemmer, U. Management support of innovative company founders. Six Countries Programme, Limerick Workshop, 1980.

OECD. The role of venture capital in the growth of information, computer and communications industries. Paris, 1984.

Office of Federal Procurement Policy. Small firms and Federal R & D. Washington, 1977.

Ogilvy, J. A. Social issues and trends: the maturation of America. Stanford Research Institute, 1984. Research Report No. 697.

Pavitt, K. Technical innovation and industrial development. Futures, Dec. 1979, 458 — 470.

Peters, T. J. *and* Waterman, R. H. In search of excellence. New York, Harper & Row, 1982.

Piattier, A. Barriers to innovation in European Community countries. C.E.C., 1981.

Porat, M. U. Communication policy in an information society. *In* Robinson, G. O. *ed.* Communications for tomorrow. Praeger, 1978.

Prakke, F. New technology based firms in the Netherlands. Six Countries Programme, Limerick Workshop, 1980.

Reich, R. The next American frontier. New York, Times Books, 1983.

Roberts, E. B. Business planning in the start-up high-technology enterprise. *In* Hornaday, J. A. *and others.* Frontiers of entrepreneurship research, 1983. Babson College, 1983.

Rothwell, R. Design matters more than price. Design, Jan. 1983.

Rotter, J. B. Generalised expectancies for internal versus external control of reinforcement. Psychological Monographs, 1966.

Sawyer, J. E. Entrepreneurial studies: perspectives and directions, 1948 — 1958. Business History Review, Winter 1985.

Schumpeter, J. Capitalism, socialism and democracy. Harvard University, 1934.

Seeman, M. *and* Evans, J. W. Alienation and learning in a hospital setting. American Sociological Review, 27, 1962.

Shackle, G. L. S. Concluding comment. Chapter IX of: Carter, C. F., Meredith, G. P. *and* Shackle, G. L. S. *eds.* Uncertainty and business decisions. Liverpool University Press, 1962.

Shapero, A. A. An action programme of entrepreneurship. Austin, MDRI Press, 1971.

Shapero, A. A. The displaced, uncomfortable entrepreneur. Psychology Today, Nov. 1975.

Shapero, A. A. The entrepreneur, the small firm and possible policies: a summing up. Six Countries Programme, Limerick Workshop, 1980.

Shapero, A. A. The management of information: the role of communication. Milan, International Institute of Technology, 1973.

Shapero, A. A. The management of professionals. (to be published 1984).

Shapero, A. A. The process of technical company formation in a local area. *In* Cooper, A. C. *and* Komives, J. L. Technical entrepreneurship: a symposium. Milwaukee, Center for Venture Management, 1972.

Shapero, A. A. The role of entrepreneurship in economic development at the less than national level. Washington, Department of Commerce, 1977.

Shapero, A. A. The role of the financial institutions of a community in the formation, effectiveness and expansion of innovating companies. Small Business Administration, 1983.

Shapero, A. A. *and* Sokol, L. The social dimensions of entrepreneurship. *In* Kent, C. A. *et al.* Encyclopaedia of entrepreneurship. New Jersey 1982.

Smith, N. R. The entrepreneur and his firm. Michigan State Univeristy, 1967.

Susbauer, J. C. The technical entrepreneurship process in Austin, Texas. *In* Cooper, A. *and* Komives, J. *eds.* Technical entrepreneurship: a symposium. Milwaukee, Center for Venture Management, 1972.

Sweeney, G. P. The future of information technology: its economic role and impact. IBM Computer Users Association Conference, York, 1980.

Sweeney, G. P. Innovation in the information economy. Six Countries Programme, Bonn Workshop, 1984.

Sweeney, G. P. New entrepreneurship and the smaller firm. IIRS, Dublin, for Six Countries Programme, 1981.

Sweeney, G. P. Technology builds people. Irish Broadcasting Review, (10) Spring 1981, 47 — 52.

Tornquist, G. Contact systems and regional development. Lund Studies, Series B (35) 1970.

Utterback, J. M. Technology and industrial innovation in Sweden. CPA, MIT and STU, Sweden, 1982.

Valecha, G. K. Construct validation of internal-external locus of reinforcement related to work-related variables. Proc. 80th Annual Convention, American Psychological Association. 7(1972).

Wolk, S. and DuCette, J. International performance and incidental learning as a function of personality and task dimensions. Journal of Personality and Social Psychology, 29, 1974.

Zschau, E. V. W. Statement before the Senate Select Committee on small business, Feb. 1978. New York, American Electronics Association, 1978.

CHAPTER 5

A new role for universities in technological innovation?

Dr. Rikard Stankiewicz

Universities are storehouses of knowledge, and in an age when knowledge takes on the characteristics of a commodity the role of the university becomes more of an economic one. Yet the normal process of transfer of knowledge from the academic to the industrial system is slow. Dr. Stankiewicz reviews the various mechanisms for promoting university-industry cooperation and suggests that successful cooperation depends on the simultaneous presence of several different kinds of exchange. No single scheme is likely to be consistently successful.

Rikard Stankiewicz, PhD, directs the R & D systems programme at the Research Policy Institute of the University of Lund, Sweden. He has conducted extensive research on the conditions of effectiveness of research teams and on the communication patterns in science and technology. His recent work focuses on the development of science-based technologies. Several case studies of such technologies are at present conducted at the RPI in Lund. The analysis of university-industry interactions constitutes a prominent feature of these studies.

New patterns of industry-university interaction

It is widely recognised today that universities play a crucial role in promoting technical change. For the most part, they make their contributions indirectly by advancing the frontiers of science, critically reviewing and systematizing accumulated technical knowledge and, especially, through the training of students and researchers.

Universities can also be viewed as pools of technical expertise and creativity to be tapped directly through the involvement of academic scientists and engineers in the process of industrial innovation. The emphasis on such direct links has been intensified in recent years. Governments, universities and industry itself have engaged in a wide spectrum of organisational experiments aiming at strengthening the links between the academic and industrial environment.

Industry-university relations are of course influenced by the recent worldwide economic slowdown. In order to improve their competitive position on stagnating or even contracting markets, nations have to mobilise all their scientific and technological resources. Universities are seen as an underutilised resource, whose contribution can be increased by adopting appropriate policies.

Universities are also asked to contribute to the structural revitalisation of national economies by assisting small and medium enterprises as well as by generating entirely new high-technology businesses. The regional importance of universities is often stressed in this connection. There is a new willingness on the part of academics to engage in various forms of service to industry, a willingness which — at least partially — can be attributed to budgetary constraints imposed on the universities by hard pressed governments.

The reasons for the current interest in university-industry relations transcend the merely conjunctural consideration, and can be linked to certain major changes in the nature of the innovation process itself. These changes started a long time ago but it is only recently that their full impact has begun to be felt.

It is hard to point to a period in history when technology underwent as rapid and many-sided a change as it is doing today. What is particularly striking is the confluence and synergistic interaction of many new basic technologies in fields as diverse as electronics, computer science, materials sciences, energy research, biotechnology, medical technology and many others. Another conspicuous characteristic of those technologies is their 'scientification' which manifests itself in:

- the sensitivity to events taking place at the frontiers of fundamental research;
- a high degree of intellectual codification and 'academisation' (as opposed to the unsystematic empiricistic character of many traditional techniques); and
- a growing intellectual complexity calling for the cooperation of people with highly specialised scientific and technological backgrounds.

As a result, the nature of the 'transactions' in which the universities engage with society at large is undergoing change. Whether they want it or not, the universities find themselves playing the role of important economic actors not only in some diffuse long-term perspective but also in a much more tangible every-day manner. Knowledge has become a commodity.

The trend toward 'scientification' of technology also calls for a readjustment of the role played by universities within the large national R & D systems. Universities are increasingly looked to as a natural integrator of the multifaceted and rapidly growing knowledge industry. They are the natural centre in which and around which the diverse specialised members of the knowledge industry cluster.

It seems inevitable that the university will undergo a variety of institutional adjustments. Many of the organisational experiments now taking place at the university-industry interface can be viewed as harbingers of more fundamental changes under way.

It is often argued that the indirect knowledge transfers between universities and industry (those mediated by the process of education, and the open communication system of science) are quite effective and do not need to be supplemented by more direct relationships to any significant extent. Universities — it is asserted — should concentrate on their primary goal, which is the expanding of our common knowledge pool, and leave the transfer and application of knowledge to other systems more suited for the purpose. These views can be supported by various quantitative indicators which show the apparent unimportance of direct university-industry links.

The belief in the ability of universities to spin off new high technology industries has also been challenged. This belief is largely based on the highly publicised success of two industrial academic complexes in the United States: route 128 and the Stanford area. A study by Sibru et al. (1976) suggested that these two examples were quite unique, and that the participation of universities in the other industrial high technology agglomerates has been quite marginal.

Yet the statistical evidence is by no means straightforward and there exist a number of studies assigning to the universities a truly significant role as contributors to technical innovation. What is the true position?

This is not the place to subject these studies to detailed review and methodological criticism. I shall therefore only point to a few general issues with direct bearing on the subject matter of the present report.

Firstly, most of the studies referred to above have been based on the assumption that the links between science and technology could be adequately measured by studying certain types of 'critical events' in science and technology ('discoveries', 'breakthroughs', 'communication of crucial ideas', etc.). This kind of 'atomistic' view is debatable. Both science and technology are intellectual systems which interact fairly continuously. The impacts which they make on one another are often the result of small and subtle influences which, nevertheless, tend to accumulate over time. Consequently, the isolation of 'critical events' or identification of supposedly crucial 'information sources' tends to be methodologically dubious.

Secondly, there is a tendency in the studies to lump together all sorts of technical innovations. This has two consequences: (i) technologically trivial innovations are not distinguished from significant ones, and/or (ii) few efforts are made to distinguish among various types of innovation processes. There is too much concern with producing some overall measure of the impact of basic science/universities on the aggregate called 'industrial innovations' and too little concern with the definition of the unique role that the universities and fundamental science have to play in technological change.

Thirdly, many of these studies lack a historical perspective. They tell us very little about whether or not and how the relationship between science and technology is changing over time.

Finally, but perhaps most importantly, they tell us very little about the actual *mechanisms of interaction* between science and technology. Consequently the correlations reported are hard to interpret.

Let us disregard for the moment the question of reliability and validity of the measures used in those studies and ask: are the low levels of interaction between universities and industry, reported by several authors, a result of the objective lack of links between science and technology or a consequence of the organisational mismatch between universities and industry?

From the policy point of view this is a crucial question. Is the scarcity of university-industry interactions an argument for doing nothing, or for redoubling our efforts?

The forging of links between science and technology proceeds along two paths. One could be called the path of *internalisation of science* within the industrial system. The second, which now has to be considered, involves the *internalisation of technology* in the academic system.

The introduction of industrial technology into the academic system is a relatively new phenomenon which historically paralleled the internalisation of science by industry. The original role of various schools of engineering (at different levels) was to collect, systematise and disseminate existing technical know-how. They were not particularly creative in terms of developing new technology or of science. That situation started changing in the second half of the 19th century. Many technical universities created at that time (such as the German Technische Hochschulen) were programatically devoted to the linking of science to applications in various fields of industry and commerce.

University trained scientists appointed to teaching positions at technical schools tended to reshape their teaching disciplines along models taken from the natural sciences. Soon the teaching in certain basic sciences became recognised as a necessary component of an engineer's education. The step from there to actual R & D activities was quite short. Especially during the first half of this century, many engineering schools both in Europe and America established important research laboratories with varying objectives and orientations.

The academic technologists contributed to the creation of technological disciplines which in some respects resembled the classical scientific ones. They placed the technological know-how on the foundations of the scientific know why. Thus the emergence of scientific-engineering hybrid disciplines systematised and institutionalised the science-technology link. Engineering departments have become important counterparts of the multi-disciplinary industrial laboratories. Together they have created a range of applied sciences which play a crucial role in the process of technological innovation (see Layton 1977).

During and after World War II the engineering schools, particularly in the USA, increased in importance due to the advent of governmental technology development programmes. Although many such programmes (especially in Europe) have been located in specially created institutions, often entirely separated from the academic system, a significant number were directly or indirectly associated with universities, especially with their engineering schools. Such programmes contributed greatly to the status of the engineering schools involved, which now could be viewed as creative contributors to technology rather than mere systematisers and disseminators.

Despite all these developments the direct links between academic technology and industry continued to be relatively limited. For example, while it is true that nearly 50 per cent of industrially sponsored research at American universities is concentrated in the engineering fields, the share of such research in the R & D activities of an average engineering department is as low as 6 — 10 per cent (NSF 1982).

The smaller and newer technical universities are more industry-oriented than their established counterparts.

To sum up, since the middle of the 19th century, science and technology have interacted vigorously. At certain times, these interactions involved direct and intense contacts between the universities and industry — as was the case with parts of chemical technology in the early stages of its development. However, such direct contacts tended gradually to be weakened and eventually superseded by the process of 'internalisation of science' within industry and the internalisation of technology at the universities.

Langrish (1974) proposes that

- after the original breakthroughs which establish a new discipline, the interests of industrial and university researchers tend to diverge, and
- once industry has built up its own R & D organisation, its dependence on the academic scientists gradually diminishes.

These hypotheses are quite consistent with the picture which emerges from Meyer-Thurow's analysis in his essay 'The Industrialisation of Invention: a Case Study from the German Chemicals Industry (1982).

Indeed, some observers seem to regard the intensive direct links between science and industry as essentially anomalous and transient phenomena. Thus Joshua Lederberg, a well-known biochemist, has expressed the opinion that the prominent role played at present by academic scientists in developing biotechnology will soon be over as the large companies establish their inhouse research laboratories.

Limits to the internalisation of science in industry

There are limits to how far the process of internalisation can be pushed. The most important of these limits are related to:

- the problems of handling basic science in an industrial environment;
- the growing complexity of industrial R & D;
- the slowness of industrial response to certain types of technical change;

- the problems with linking academic technology to the specific needs of industry;
- the slowness of science-transfer through education, and
- the problem of low R & D sophistication of many small and middle size firms.

The most advanced form of internalisation of science in industry is the initiation of basic research programmes in industrial laboratories. This development seems to have culminated in the late 50s. From the 60s onwards, the proportion of industrial R & D investments devoted to basic research in the USA had decreased from 8 to 4 per cent (NSF 1978). Similar tendencies have developed in the European industries (OECD 1980). Other explanations include a growing general distrust of a 'technology push' philosophy, low corporate profitability, regulations discouraging radical innovation, relative absence of radical scientific and technological breakthroughs, changes in managerial styles, excessive concentration of R & D resources in defensive programmes, etc.

At the same time there occurred an apparent weakening of the role of industry in the financing of academic research, though this was probably due more to expansion of government support for basic research rather than to a decline in industrial support.

NSF figures from 1982 indicate that the funds flowing from industry to university research increased not only in absolute terms but also in terms of their relative importance in the overall financing of academic research (NSF 1982).

Thus, we seem to be experiencing two contradictory tendencies. On the one hand, an apparent decrease in long-term R & D and basic research in industry itself and, on the other, a steady growth of industrial support to academic research at least in the U.S. How does one account for this paradox?

The simple explanation is that, while becoming increasingly aware of the importance of basic research for technological innovation, industry realises more and more clearly its own limitations in this sphere. With a few spectacular exceptions, the industrial research laboratories have not proved themselves to be good environments for the pursuit of fundamental science. Many companies have therefore started to seek direct links to the universities and to use their inhouse basic R & D as transmission mechanisms.

The more 'scientified' a technology becomes, the more sensitive it is to what happens on the frontiers of science. As the technological competition intensifies, companies seek more effective means of staying abreast of the developments in basic technologies. That sets a premium on quick direct links to the universities.

A second factor is the growing complexity of technological change. More and more of the emerging technologies require knowledge inputs from a large number of scientific and technological disciplines.

Even the largest companies find it difficult to maintain sufficiently diversified internal R & D resources to stay self sufficient. Instead, they become more dependent on highly diversified external sources of knowledge.

While the technological potential of universities, particularly technical ones, increases there is a growing concern with its effective utilisation. As already noted, many of the most advanced technology development programmes located in the universities have been government sponsored. Their focus has often been on military, strategic or welfare problems. It is now felt that a better coupling needs to be established between academic technology and private industry. This can hardly be achieved without intensified direct interactions between the two environments.

In most cases, the indirect transfer mechanisms (i.e. those mediated by the educational process) tend to be slow. It has been suggested (Price, 1964) that the great time lags which frequently occur in the technological utilisation of the results of scientific research are due precisely to the slowness with which scientific knowledge becomes incorporated in engineering education. Worse still, academic technology often lags behind the developments in the more advanced companies. In order to teach relevant skills, academic teachers must be exposed to relevant research. In rapidly advancing areas of technology, this can be achieved only when there is a high degree of direct coupling between academic and industrial R & D.

The last area where the indirect mode of interaction between universities and industry appears to be unsatisfactory is one of technology transfer to small and medium-sized enterprises. The larger the company, the more likely it is to interact *directly or indirectly* with universities. In the U.K. the Universities and Industry Joint Committee (1970) found that there was a positive correlation between firm size and the use of universities as the source of knowledge inputs to technological innovation. This suggests that the direct and indirect links between universities and industry are complementary. The presence of inhouse R & D capability is a decisive factor in a company's ability to utilise external sources of knowledge (whether through direct or indirect links). That puts the small and middle size companies in a position of disadvantage.

These facts notwithstanding, it is widely believed that the universities could play the role of a substitute for internal R & D in small companies. That implies very intimate contacts between the universities and the firms involved. While such contacts may be hard to establish, it is argued that the effort is worth its costs because of the greater innovativeness of the small companies. Much of the recent concern with the university-industry relationship focuses on this issue.

The available evidence concerning the role and significance of university-industry interactions is unclear and full of contradictions. At least from the middle of the 19th century, science exercised an important impact on industry. For the most part, the integration of science and technology took place either in the industry's own laboratories or in the engineering departments of universities. The direct university-industry links (such as joint R & D projects, extensive utilisation of academic scientists and engineers in the industrial programme etc.), with relatively few exceptions, seemed to play a very modest role.

The relative balance between the indirect and direct links between universities and industry is now beginning to change. The processes of 'internalisation' of science by industry and of 'academisation' of technology at the universities have their natural limits which become increasingly obvious as more and more technology is put on a scientific basis. The so-called 'high technologies' rapidly change from being isolated islands on the industrial maps into large archipelagos or even continents. As the result of these developments the traditional means of linking science and technology become strained and require modifications.

Universities as sources of R & D assistance to industry

The most common type of direct university-industry link involves the participation of academic scientists/engineers in technology development activities initiated and managed by industrial firms. In such cases the overall entrepreneurial responsibility rests with the sponsoring company while the academics act in highly specialised technical roles.

Even large and sophisticated companies may find the process of identifying areas of fruitful collaboration with universities both time consuming and costly. In order to achieve appropriate matching of interests between universities and industry a long-term strategy is needed on both sides. The process of communications has to be established and function well before specific projects can get under way. Even granted that the industrial demands and university potential have been properly matched, there still remains the problem of establishing an appropriate organisation for carrying out joint activities. Experience shows that in order to minimise such pitfalls it is necessary to evolve a whole range of complementary university-industry interfaces.

Consulting

Consultancy by academic scientists and engineers is the most frequently occurring, versatile and cost-effective means of linking industry with university. According to one survey

(Marver and Patton, 1976), about one third of the faculty at American universities have been engaged in various forms of consultancy. According to the data presented by the U.K. Universities and Industry Joint Committee (1970) academic consultants have been used by roughly 70 per cent of large companies (with employment of 5,000 and over) and nearly 50 per cent of companies employing 500 to 5,000 people.

This is a relatively inexpensive, rapid and selective means of transferring information. In so far as it rarely involves extensive demands on university personnel and material resources it leads to few institutional tensions. Furthermore, consultants can fulfil a very broad range of functions. They can be used as 'trouble shooters' when a company is facing a special difficulty of some kind, or as advisers helping a company to evaluate its own projects and ideas. They can also serve as gate-keepers to the wider scientific community. They can provide industry with information on a broad spectrum of problems from basic research to commercial assessment of products. Industry sponsored projects carried out at universities tend to be established on the basis of previous consulting arrangements (Culliton, 1983).

What makes consultancy so important is that it constitutes probably the most effective two-way communication channel between university and industry. Academic scientists and engineers who engage in consultancy acquire a knowledge of the needs of industry and can therefore identify the specific ways in which these needs can be met by their universities.

Particularly significant in this context are long-term consultancies as opposed to simple 'trouble shooting'.

The expansion and improvement of consultancy links should be regarded as the necessary first step in the process of stimulating direct university-industry links.

In Europe, the personal links between companies and university departments seem to be particularly well developed in Germany, Switzerland, Holland and the Scandinavian countries. They are weaker in other European countries such as France, Italy and Spain (OECD, 1972). The process of interaction between universities and industry is self-reinforcing

— it intensifies with time. Even though nowadays everybody advocates improved university-industry links, some countries, notably Germany and the USA, have a lead which is not easy to eliminate.

Industrially sponsored R & D in university departments

Industrially sponsored R & D within disciplinary departments represents a far more problematic university-industry link than does ordinary consultancy. The sources of conflict and inefficiency are numerous.

Although the various disciplinary departments of universities do often have much to offer in terms of R & D expertise, they are not very flexible in adapting to industry's demands. This rigidity is caused by certain institutional imperatives rather than bad management or the culturally determined 'ivory-towerism'. The effective utilisation of the potential locked in the university department depends therefore on the industry's ability to tailor its own demands so as to make them compatible with the constraints under which academic scientists and engineers are forced to work.

The costs in time and effort required discourage many companies, particularly the small ones, from searching for academic partners. Up to a point this can be remedied with the help of various 'broker' arrangements.

Liaison offices

Government-sponsored liaison units have been in operation for years in the United Kingdom, France, Federal Republic of Germany, Sweden and other countries. These units differ considerably among themselves in the resources they command, their functions and location. For instance, while the Swedish units are linked administratively to the universities, the French liaison offices are situated in various industrial research assocations (Rothwell, 1982). Many of the earliest liaison centres tended to be limited to the transmission of information while those started more recently usually have a more complex profile. While most liaison units have a very broad character, there are also instances of highly specialised ones. In some countries efforts are being made to regionalise the liaison function. As an example of this one can take the Dutch 'transfer points' discussed during the Stockholm meeting.

There is a growing consensus on the conditions under which liaison units can be made effective.

- liaison units should be located within the university structure; it is essential that the local officers are intimately familiar with the departments and their activities;
- it is crucial that the officers are perceived as competent, particularly by the scientific community; careful recruitment is therefore decisive; mistakes are as a rule hard to correct;
- in order to achieve the right sort of recruitment, it is important that the liaison function has high visibility and status within the university structure;
- the liaison units should adopt an active marketing approach rather than a passive service-when-demanded approach;
- the liaison function should, preferably, be linked to other interface mechanisms (such as research institutes, technology transfer units, or research parks) rather than operate entirely on their own.

University-industry consortia

The liaison offices (and consulting companies) offer their services on the open market. There exist however far more specialised forms of industry-university brokers. Consortia are sometimes formed by groups of companies to establish collective links to a university or a group of universities.

Consortia of this sort are created chiefly to promote applied research. When it comes to the industrial support of more basic research within universities another method is sometimes used. It involves the creation by one or several companies of a 'foundation' or institute which distributes the money to individual researchers and departments.

An example of this kind is provided by the Semi-conductor Research Cooperative which has been established to pool funds from U.S. electronics companies for support to basic research at universities. The scheme originally proposed by IBM now has several participating companies. The idea is that each member company will have access to all the SRC-sponsored research (Norman, 1982).

Arrangements of this sort have the advantage of creating a very intimate long-term link between industry and university. This can be effective in bringing about the appropriate matching of the industry's needs with the opportunities offered by the universities. Unfortunately this kind of arrangement appears to work well only when relatively few highly sophisticated companies are involved. We shall return to this theme when discussing the so-called university-industry centre for cooperative research.

The limitations of academic departments as partners in university-industry interaction

Given the fact that the R & D resources of a university are located almost exclusively within the disciplinary departments the direct links between them and industry would seem to be of paramount importance. However, as was pointed out earlier in this report these direct links are subject to severe constraints. Simplifying matters somewhat one might say that there are only three kinds of direct department-industry cooperation that do not necessarily create acute problems. These are:

- Consultancies requiring a relatively limited amount of time on the part of the academics involved, in which the advice sought is usually of a highly specific character; when a company needs a blend of technical and commercial advice (something which is often the case especially with smaller companies) hiring of academic advisers may be less satisfactory.
- Research projects which are long-term in character, capable of being handled by a single discipline and,

preferably, pose a genuine intellectual challenge in terms of disciplinary criteria. In addition, the projects should not be of a size which can excessively affect the research profile/direction of the department. Short-term problem solving contract research, or large multidisciplinary efforts go against the grain of the academic structure.

● Research projects which are relatively free of secrecy and in which no serious problems regarding proprietary rights are likely to emerge.

While the removal of unnecessary 'red-tape' and establishment of appropriate 'rules of the game' will help things, one must not push them too far. The research activities of academic departments must ultimately be governed by disciplinary standards.

And yet to limit the university-industry interactions to things that can easily be fitted to the departmental structure is not a realistic solution either. This is particularly true of the relations with smaller companies which cannot be as flexible in defining their demands as are the large R & D intensive companies.

Extra-departmental 'Interface' structures

In order to overcome difficulties of this sort universities have been adding to their structure a variety of 'interface' organisations and systems designed to deal with industrial contracts not easily handled within the departmental system.

They differ from the simple 'broker' arrangements which were discussed above in that they go significantly beyond the pure go-between functions. They *themselves* accept responsibility for meeting the needs of the industrial client.

The interfaces have the following main functions:

(1) They constitute legal entities which are distinct from departments capable of entering into contractual arrangements which would be difficult or impossible for regular departments.

(2) As a rule they maintain some technical staff of their own and thus are able to respond to requests not

readily met by scientists and engineers from the disciplinary departments. Their staff possess R & D and commercial skills which are complementary to those of the universities.

(3) Most interface organisations possess their own laboratories/equipment or have regular access to the laboratory space and equipment of the university. They can thus provide premises and resources for carrying out contract R & D.

Applied research institutes are a classical form of university-industry interface. They are designed to handle contract research. The institutes have as a rule large multidisciplinary resources and managerial structures which are well adapted to the needs of industrial clients. They are usually capable of handling both small and large R & D projects and are often capable of mobilising considerable resources within a short period of time — something which is usually impossible for ordinary academic departments. The presence of an applied research institute at a university creates a base for a truly effective liaison function. The system is particularly well developed in the German Federal Republic.

The range and character of services offered by institutes varies considerably. Some institutes, such as SINTEF in Norway, offer a broad range of technical services. Other institutes may have highly specialised functions either in terms of technology or of industrial sector.

Seen from our point of view the effectiveness of the institutes is a function of the degree of linkage they can establish with the rest of universities. When they fail to maintain such linkage to a significant degree they will 'degenerate' to the same status as private contract research laboratories or the 'branch laboratories' of industrial associations.

Their particular strength is that they can handle problems on the basis of bilateral contracts with individual companies. They are therefore well suited to do work where secrecy and proprietary work are a major dimension and which has to be carried out under conditions approximating those found in industry. As an organisational framework however, they are not necessarily the only or the best means of handling more fundamental types of technological R & D.

University-industry cooperative research centres

By cooperative research centres we mean those arrangements where the participating companies become associated with a university affiliated R & D operation on a long-term basis rather than on a project basis. This form of university-industry interface has recently become quite popular in the United States, largely thanks to the initiatives of the NSF.

A central feature of a cooperative research centre (CRC) is that it has as a rule only a limited number of sponsoring companies (sometimes just one).

This distinguishes it from the European style collective research institutes which are usually run by branch associations. CRCs may be regarded as logical extensions of department-based industrially sponsored *research projects* involving one or (more often) several companies. They are particularly well adapted to the needs of long-term development in the area of basic or generic technologies.

The simplest form of a CRC is the one company — one university arrangement. This can be illustrated by the agreement between Hoechst AG and the Harvard Medical School to set up within the school a Department of Molecular Biology. The department does not, strictly speaking, belong to the school; rather it is affiliated with the school, the linkage taking chiefly the form of personal union (Culliton, 1982).

This sort of arrangement tends to be controversial because it threatens to obliterate the distinction between the regular departmental system and the interface system. Some scientists are worried that it is a subtle way of gradually subordinating basic research to commercial interest.

The case described above illustrates the desire of industry to plug into the best academic research environments in the fields of related biotechnology. In return for their often generous support the companies hope to acquire a 'window' on the research front, access to the flow of scientific talent, opportunity to acquire a sophisticated network of consultants, and the right (preferably exclusive) to such inventions as may be generated in the course of research supported by them. These arragements are important complements to the companies' own long term research programmes. One of the conditions of their success is however that a strong linkage is established between such centres and the companies' own *inhouse* activities. Linkage is usually provided by placing the company's own scientists and engineers in the centres. The idea is to create both a permanent communication channel and to train their own R & D personnel.

Roughly the same is true of the collaborative research centres sponsored by several companies simultaneously. In the United States several such centres have been established on an experimental basis under the auspices of the NSF.

Reviewing the conditions of success Colton (1981) emphasises the following points:

- the success of the centres depends largely on the presence of a strong and dynamic leader;
- the centres must enjoy strong and direct support of the university and industry; the government should play the role of a midwife but should not interfere with the management of the centres;
- the centres do best when they focus on a combination of basic and applied research;

  'The most successful centres were involved in general areas of science and technology, and innovation that cut across industry lines; for example, computer or polymer technology as opposed to furniture or offshore technology.' (Ibid).

This last point requires special emphasis. The concept of university-industry centre is quite different from that of a 'branch institute' in that: the cooperation takes place in an area of high technology; the participating companies are relatively few and tend to operate in different markets. The focus on 'generic' technology, which is characteristic for the CRCs, makes it easier for the participating companies to cooperate; it is also fairly compatible with academic values.

The conditions required for the centres to be effective seem to be:

- The ability to bring about effective collaboration between relevant fields/departments which in turn requires formulation of a programme concept which can intellectually mobilise the resources dispersed throughout the departmental structure of the university.
- The ability to identify genuine areas of generic technology such that a coherent coalition of companies prepared to back them can be put together. Both these conditions require imagination and a great deal of footwork.

General Assistance Units (GAU)

The interface organisations which are to serve the needs of small and middle-size companies have to be based on quite different principles than those applying to the CRCs discussed above. In recent years several attempts have been made to achieve that by setting up what may be called the 'general assistance units'.

Just as the industry-university cooperative centres might be viewed as extensions of research financing consortia or enlargements of industrially sponsored projects at univerisities, the GAUs can be seen as further developments of liaison offices and university affiliated consulting companies.

The philosophy of GAUs is that most companies — in any case most of the small or middle size companies — require multiple forms of assistance. Such assistance may be impossible to obtain from individual academic departments — no matter how effective the broker functions. Liaison officers often discover that it is easier to sell academic research to companies when it is offered as a 'package' including, in addition to strictly technical services, such other things as administrative help, patent advice, help with licensing arrangements, market assessment, financial planning, etc. Consequently experiments are being conducted in several countries with new types of organisational units capable of providing this form of multifaceted assistance.

In some respects these programmes come close to the so-called 'innovation centres' which will be discussed later. People who run them emphasise the entrepreneurial-managerial aspects of the assistance they render. This feature makes the GAUs attractive but at the same time involves certain risks. On the positive side is the fact that there seems to be a market for services of this kind. In fact there have been several recent attempts to exploit that market by private companies unconnected with universities. For example, the American company, Control Data Corporation, has started several business and technology centres which offer to small companies a whole range of services including R & D, secretarial sources, data bank, communication facilities, and advice in such matters as cash management, accounting, marketing and law (*Financial Times,* July 27, 1982). One such centre has been opened in Twente, the Netherlands, apparently with an eye on possible collaboration with the scientists and engineers of the technical university of Overijssel.

The competitive advantage which the universities have over private initiatives in providing such general assistance to companies rests chiefly on the breadth of the academic R & D resources. What is more questionable is their ability to mobilise the sort of managerial and entrepreneurial skills that are required. Consequently the centres must draw on the resources of the entrepreneurial and financial community just as they do on the resources of the university.

Research parks

Physical proximity is often regarded as an important factor contributing to enhanced university-industry interaction. Indeed, many examples can be cited of intensive interaction between universities and local companies. For example, the Swedish pharmaceutical concern Fortia is known to base its R & D strategy on close links to the University of Uppsala. The

British company Tate and Lyle operates a laboratory at the campus of the University of Reading. This sort of physical closeness can be expected to facilitate intellectual osmosis between industry and universities. Research or science parks are one of the means of stimulating this osmosis. The idea is to create in the vicinity of universities sufficient room for the small high-technology companies and the R & D laboratories of larger ones. It is hoped that this will lead to the development of dense networks of informal contacts, consultancies and joint projects between the host universities and the companies in the park.

Science parks have been a mixed success both commercially and in terms of promoting university-industry interaction. We shall discuss them in greater detail later on.

There are many different types of 'science parks'. Some are run by universities themselves, some by local governments and still others are purely private. The industrial tenants of the science parks are as a rule the mobile R & D laboratories/ projects of established companies, small high-technology companies with R & D as a dominant activity, various types of research institutes, etc.

The idea of science parks originated in the United States after the Second World War. Perhaps the most famous among the pioneering schemes was the Stanford Industrial Park, started in 1947 thanks to the effort of Frederick E. Terman.

At present there are over 80 science parks in the U.S. and about 20 in the U.K. New parks are being started in many countries, including Ireland, the Netherlands and Sweden. What has been the relative success of these schemes?

Opinions differ, partly depending on what criteria of success are being used.

Mere physical proximity to a university is not enough. The strength of the academic R & D and the organisational links are what ultimately matter. The universities and engineering schools with a rich blend of basic and applied research will attract high technology firms, second rate universities or those indifferent to technology will not. Generally speaking, parks run by universities themselves will probably do better than those financed and managed by other interests. Indeed practically all the really great science parks have a strong university affiliation. Another prominent feature of successful parks is that they tend to function as components in larger systems of interface, rather as isolated phenomena. Indeed in some cases, the science park provides the location for other interfaces such as applied research institutes, collaborative research centres, innovation centres and the like.

Concluding comments

While the direct use of departmental resources is indispensable to industrial innovation, it will not be optimal unless reinforced by a variety of special university-industry interfaces. We have considered four types of such interfaces, including the applied research institutes, the collaborative research centres, the integrated assistance units and the science parks. Although to some extent overlapping in their functions, these interfaces all have specialised roles to play. In fact it can be argued that only the simultaneous presence of all these types of interfaces can guarantee smooth university-industry interaction. And, conversely, none of the schemes taken alone can achieve complete success.

There is considerable variation in the effectiveness with which they are being applied. For each type of interface one can cite some resounding successes, a large number of cases of middling performance, as well as some clear cut failures. This depends in part on the special historical circumstances under which the different university-industry schemes have developed. Managerial skills also appear to be an important consideration.

The university-industry interactions must be viewed as a process in which learning is the key factor. Even the best conceived structures will not produce quick results. In an indifferent or hostile environment the initial lack of success can initiate a vicious circle of diminishing support leading to further failures. In a supportive environment the prospect of successful 'debugging' of novel organisational arrangements is much more favourable.

Universities as sources of inventions and technical entrepreneurship

The ability of university scientists and engineers to succeed in the roles of inventors and technical entrepreneurs is a matter of some controversy. It is often asserted that academics, working far from the marketplace, rarely exhibit the particular mixture of commercial and technical instincts which is necessary for successful innovation. Furthermore, the nature of the inventions which are likely to emerge from universities makes technology transfer rather difficult. Academics seem more successful at creating basic (or 'generic') technologies rather than user-specific inventions. With few exceptions, such as the development of scientific instruments, the university people tend to lack the detailed knowledge of the market needs, without which the user-specific invention is not possible. Also academic technology tends to have a 'software' rather than a 'hardware' character. As such it tends to be sold as consulting services rather than as patents or physical goods.

There are several reasons for an underutilisation of universities as the source of technical ideas.

The technological-commercial implications of academic R & D are seldom self-evident. Just as one needs a prepared mind to elevate a chance observation to the status of scientific discovery, one needs it to recognise technological opportunities. Some degree of exposure to the technological needs of industry would certainly be helpful in promoting inventing activity.

The commercial worth of an idea is likewise rarely self-evident, especially at its embryonic stage. Someone must become the champion of the emerging technology treating it as a potential asset to be developed. This involves an expenditure of time, energy and other resources.

Most ideas, before they can be transferred, must be further developed. The work required will as a rule fall outside the scope of normal academic R & D. That can lead to conflicts similar to those arising in the case of applied contract R & D carried out in the academic departments.

In brief, the transfer of academic technology to the marketplace requires a sustained effort which presupposes considerable resources, both material and personal. Such resources are often lacking in the academic system. Over the years several methods have been tried out to eliminate these deficiencies. These can be grouped into three main categories:

1. Policies aiming to improve the *marketing* of academic technology. These include changes in the rules and laws governing proprietary rights to technology (patents, licence, royalties) as well as in the marketing behaviour in the strict sense.

2. Policies aiming at the creation of *broker institutions* capable of closing the development and financing gaps which often separate the academic inventors from their potential partners in industry.

3. Policies aiming to encourage *academic entrepreneurship* and to *promote the* creation of new *spin-off* firms.

The most elementary form of technology transfer consists in offering it for sale in open markets. This requires clear definition of the proprietary rights and a certain amount of active salesmanship. The practices concerning patenting of university-generated technology differ considerably from country to country and from university to university. (For a comparative survey, see Niels Reimers, 1979.)

The growing realisation of the importance of patenting of science based technologies has called for the revision of some of the existing laws and regulations.

Recent changes in U.S. legislation making it easier to patent techniques and materials in such areas as biotechnology can be viewed in this light (Blumenthal, 1983).

Although the sense of legitimacy of patenting of university-generated technology is becoming stronger, there are still many ethical issues unresolved. The major second trend as regards patenting concerns the development of new codes of conduct for patenting the results of scientific research. Among emerging features of such a code are: the preference for non-exclusive licensing of generic technologies, the practice of channelling the proceeds from patents back to research, and the experiments with collective rather than individual ownership of patents. This last policy aims at minimising the striving towards secrecy and commercial rivalry among members of the same laboratory/department.

The *third trend* affecting the patenting of university-generated technology involves changes in the ideas about just *who* should assume the responsibility for the exploitation of the patents. Established rules have tended to be biased in favour of the financial sponsors, for the most part the governments. This bias was due partly to the idea that inventions made with the help of public funds should also be publicly owned and partly to the notion that governments were in a better position to exploit the patents than were the academics. As witnessed by the recent legislative changes in the USA and the U.K. both these ideas have come to be seriously questioned. At present the trend seems to be in the direction of vindicating the rights of individual inventors and the universities.

By giving a university a commercial stake in the technology created by its scientists one can hope to establish technological innovation as an integral function of the academic system. An arrangement of this kind can help to establish in the public mind a *symbiotic* relationship between academic science and technology.

Licensing offices

According to several studies cited by Shapero (1979) very few patents held by universities show returns.

> 'As a source of patents and licences obtained by companies, universities rank a low third behind companies in other fields and private research laboratories.'

Despite such doubts many universities both in the United States and in Europe have found it useful to set up special units charged with the responsibility of licensing commercial technology resulting from their scientists' research activities. Normally these are very minor operations within a university's administration, occasionally delegatd to an industrial liaison officer or a contract research institute. There exist, however, instances of much more ambitious schemes, such as the Wisconsin Alumni Research Foundation in the United States (Reimers, 1980). The management of patent-portfolios rarely yields large incomes. When they do materialise such incomes are usually the fruit of one or a few highly successful patents which would be exploited no matter who manages them. It seems therefore that the academic patent licensing offices, even when profitable to the universities operating them, cannot really be regarded as important means of technology transfer from universities to industry. They will succeed where success is easy and fail where things are more difficult. Licensing offices and similar organisations are generally not in the position to assume the full entrepreneurial responsibility for the technology they wish to promote.

Long term licensing arrangements between industry and universities

An alternative method of marketing academic technology is to offer individual companies or groups of companies patent rights or licences on the inventions produced by the university scientists in some defined area of R & D. This is usually done in return for research support provided by the companies. Several of the cooperative research programmes discussed previously give the companies involved the right to technology which might be developed in the course of research programmes they support at the universities. The Harvard-Monsanto agreement, to take one example, gives the company the patent rights for inventions and applications from the research it sponsors on the TAF (Tumor Angrogenesis Factor) (Culliton, 1977).

Arrangements of this kind are, of course, by no means unique to the field of biotechnology. For example: Exxon Research and Engineering Company has linked with MIT in the area of combustion science.

But there also exist some serious objections to such schemes. First of all it seems hardly appropriate that individual companies are given exclusive rights to the technologies developed at universities. For that reason the tendency is to favour arrangements in which the universities hold the patents and the companies involved receive non-exclusive royalty-free licences to these patents (compare Colton, 1981).

Another objection to the special university-company relationship is that those arrangements onesidedly favour sophisticated high-tech companies with large own R & D resources. Smaller companies, lacking the financial strength or/and technical sophistication necessary to cultivate 'special relationships' with leading universities, would thus be put in a position of disadvantage.

It is difficult at present to evaluate the real advantages and disadvantages of the 'special arrangements'. The schemes discussed above are too few and too recent. But, if the trend towards more cooperative research continues, the pattern of swapping of research support for technological spin-offs may become an important feature of the university-industry interface. For this reason its legal and institutional features require close scrutiny.

Innovation brokers

As governments' investment in R & D has increased, so has the concern with the effective utilisation of the results emerging from it. In many countries there has been a feeling that the technologies developed in governmental laboratories and at universities have not been transferred to civilian industry to a sufficient extent. To alter this state of affairs special bodies have been set up, the best known being NRDC in the U.K. and ANVAR in France. Following Reimers we shall call these schemes 'National Research and Development Organisations' (NRDOs).

What distinguishes NRDOs from the university licensing offices is, firstly, the fact that they operate on the national level and have vastly superior personnel and material resources.

Secondly, they are in the position to actively *push* the utilisation of academic technology by organising development programmes and providing risk capital.

One argument for the formation of NRDOs has been the belief that many potentially important university inventions require further development and championing before they could become attractive to industry. The hypothesis is that there often appears to be a 'development gap' which neither universities nor private companies are willing to fill. When this happens a NRDO would be expected to step in.

As pointed out by Rothwell (1982) it is very difficult to adequately assess the performance of NRDOs. When the relationships between universities and industry are poorly developed the national research development organisations will perforce have an important role to play. However, to quote Rothwell:

> 'From the viewpoint of the inventor himself,.....,, it is possible   to identify a number of frequently voiced complaints. These are: risk-aversion, bureaucratic procedures and over-lengthy decision- making processes.'

Indeed in some instances, the apparent successes of these bodies turn out, on closer examination, to be somewhat dubious. The astounding rate of success (90 per cent!) claimed by the Japanese Research Development Corporation suggests that few risks are taken (compare Moritani, M., Japanese Technology, Tokyo 1982, p.182). Indeed one suspects that NRDOs, like the university licensing offices, succeed best where success is easy, i.e. whenever the technology is such that it immediately attracts a dynamic and resourceful entrepreneur from established industry.

University-run development companies

Although many universities have owned land and industrial stock as a source of income, the actual running of businesses based on the results of research performed by the university's own scientists and engineers is as rare as it is controversial. Yet there are examples where such operations have been quite successful. L'Institute Pasteur in France established in 1972 a 'captive company' which manufactures and sells products based on technology developed at the institute. Despite the fact that a large proportion of the patents held by it are being exploited to other firms, the institute appears to regard its production company as an important part of its technology transfer activities (Reimers, 1980).

The pros and cons of the universities assumming the role of technical entrepreneurs have been recently debated in the United States. While some universities, including Harvard, decided against running their own companies, others, such as Berkeley and Stanford, adopted a much more positive attitude.

As in the case of 'special relationships' between universities and individual firms, little can be said at this point about the effectiveness of the university run development companies. It is difficult to envisage a situation in which such companies could become a common occurrence at universities. The institutional and legal obstacles are too many. But neither should the university companies be dismissed out of hand. Rather we should view them as one element in the peripheral system of the university, where it might play a role in bridging the 'entrepreneurial gap' separating universities from industry.

Stimulating academic entrepreneurship

It can be argued that small, newly-created companies have a special role to play in exploiting new technologies emerging from universities. One feature of many new technologies is that in their initial stages they often develop in niches, i.e. high-price/small volume markets which, while ideal for new small businesses, are of limited interest to large established firms.

Also there is a growing recognition that technical ideas tend to die when separated from active entrepreneurs. It is quite possible that many creative ideas spun off by academics atrophy because their authors have lost interest in them at too early a stage. Roberts & Peters' observation that in the universities inventiveness and entrepreneurship do not always go together sums it up nicely.

These and similar insights have led to calls for new measures to stimulate entrepreneurial behaviour among academics. The desirability of such measures is further emphasised by pointing to certain outstanding examples of industrial creativity and expansion spearheaded or at least greatly enhanced by academic spin-off firms: particularly Silicon Valley, and Route 128. The explosive development of biotechnology, in which academic spin-off firms play the leading role, is also cited as an illustration of the role which academic entrepreneurs may come to play in promoting new science-based industries.

At the same time there exists a widespread awareness of the difficulties which the promotion of academic entrepreneurship is likely to encounter. These difficulties tend to be considerably greater than the ones associated with the university-industry interactions involving mere technical assistance. The crux of the matter is that the entrepreneurial role tends to be extremely demanding.

As the entrepreneur is the very opposite of a specialised technician or a conventional manager his role has no clear boundaries but instead expands and contracts depending on the character and the stage of development of the enterprise.

The evolution of an academic invention may be said to include three main stages. The first stage takes place in the cocoon of a department. A scientist/engineer (on or off his job) hits on an idea which he gradually develops using the technical resources available to him as a private individual or as a member of the department. This stage can continue as long as no major conflict develops between the inventor-entrepreneur and the department. Such conflicts, when they arise, usually centre around the institutional norms (legitimacy of commercial work) or around the question of resources.

The second stage could be called transitional. The scientist-inventor seeks a broader resource base than that provided by the department without, however, severing his link with the university. His entrepreneurial role becomes significantly enlarged. He will now try to solicit development resources of considerably greater scope than those commonly available at a university, or, in any case, in a single department. At this point conflicts with the department can become acute. The inventor is forced to find some other organisational base.

The third stage involves the actual commercial launching of the invention outside the university. The academic entrepreneur either starts his own firm or becomes an entrepreneur in an established company.

Naturally, a scientist-entrepreneur does not have to pass through all three phases outlined above. The technology being developed can be successfully transferred to some other user at an early stage. The trouble is however that the academic entrepreneur is liable to quit long before such transfer occurs. Why is it so and what can be done about it?

To begin with, the entrepreneurial activity is liable to run into the same kind of difficulties as the other kinds of 'applied research' at universities. There will be conflicts concerning academic norms which regulate the use of time, departmental resources, etc. Furthermore, there are likely to arise difficulties regarding inter-disciplinarity — how to provide the inventor with the necessary expertise from fields other than his own. Last but not least, there may develop serious tensions concerning the ownership rights to the technology which is being developed.

The absence of the necessary skills is at least as important an obstacle to entrepreneurship as the institutional factors. An entrepreneur is often required to act as a jack-of-all trades. He is a synthesiser rather than a specialist. The academic environment does not abound in that sort of person. A university's scientists and engineers trying to become entrepreneurs soon find themselves in unfamiliar territory.

Very few scientists and engineers in the university environment have been exposed to entrepreneurial role-models. This absence creates a sense of unfamiliarity which discourages entrepreneurship. Direct or indirect experience of entrepreneurship seems to be clearly correlated with the person's propensity to engage in it.

As a rule an academic entrepreneur finds himself in an environment which is indifferent and often hostile to him. He is a deviant rather than the hero. This lack of encouragement in combination with the unfamiliarity of the role he has to play and with the genuine uncertainties inevitably accompanying a new venture, goes a long way to explain why so few potential or actual academic inventors become successful entrepreneurs.

Becoming an entrepreneur does not necessarily mean that one quits one's academic career. A scientist or an engineer who has developed an embryonic business may sell it and then resume his regular academic career. Or he may choose to run a business as a sideline. However, those who opt for a new non-academic career face the difficult transition from a relatively sheltered academic position to a situation of self-employment. Many potential entrepreneurs may baulk at such a risky and often irreversible decision.

During the Stockholm Workshop several ways of facilitating this transition were discussed. One type of measure which could limit the risks is to grant the prospective entrepreneurs extended leave-of-absence (a sort of entrepreneurial sabbatical) during which he could test his business ideas. Furthermore, steps should be taken to assure the convertibility/transferability of pension funds and other forms of assurance which the would-be entrepreneur has acquired during his academic career.

Interface organisations: innovation centres, liaison offices, etc.

Minor adjustments in the academic rules of the game cannot solve all the problems. Other than in very exceptional cases, academic departments cannot be effective as incubators of new businesses, at least not beyond a certain point. The conflicts over institutional norms and values, the need of interdisciplinary support or the sheer magnitude of the undertaking will sooner or later force the entrepreneur to seek contacts and support outside his department. The ease with which such contacts and support can be obtained depends to a large extent on the relationship between the university and the surrounding business community, and on the presence within the university itself or in its vicinity of the appropriate mediating organisations and institutions.

Applied research institutes, university-run development and

consulting companies and research parks can all contribute to the creation of appropriate conditions for the 'hatching' of university-generated innovations. They can provide the academic inventor with the same kind of assistance as they give to non-academic entrepreneurs and small firms. It may be recalled that some of the liaison units discussed previously have specialised in assisting the spin-off firms from universities.

In this context, special attention must be paid to the so-called 'innovation centres'. Initiated in 1973 as a special programme under the auspices of the National Science Foundation in the USA, the centres have two main objectives:

(a) to contribute to the diffusion of entrepreneurial skills and value in the academic environment, and

(b) to actually help to launch new firms.

There are some variations in the organisation and mode of operation of the individual centres. However, most of them share the following features:

(i) they offer formal courses on various subjects relevant to entrepreneurship. This includes various practical exercises such as devising business plans, carrying out market research, and so on.

(ii) they assist interested inventors (usually academic) in carrying out commercial/ technical assessment of their idea (venture analysis). This often involves setting up expert panels consisting of the centre staff and students as well as other experts drawn from the university.

(iii) they assist innovators in getting the necessary contacts with potential business partners, financial institutions, and similar.

(iv) in some cases they provide the facilities and technical expertise necessary for further development of the inventions submitted by the would-be entrepreneur.

The evaluations so far carried out suggest that the centres

have enjoyed a modest success. Assessing the early performance record of the three original U.S. innovation centres in 1976, Colton and Udell (1976) found that during the first two years of their existence, the centres

- significantly increased the rate of entrepreneurship among the participating graduates;
- attracted increasing numbers of students;
- contributed to the commercialisation of twenty-five new products and procedures, and thus
- helped to create 240 jobs and $3.4 million worth in sales.

The broader educational effects of the centres' activities are of course hard to assess. It seems nevertheless fair to say that the centres have helped to expose a considerable number of academics to entrepreneurship and its culture. That may be of lesser importance in the univesities, such as MIT, which have a long tradition of close links to the entrepreneurial and business communities. In the universities not possessing such links the impact of the centres could be quite significant.

The educational importance of the centres may well depend on their ability to broaden the professional profile of students. In doing so they counter the tendency in the universities to produce narrowly specialised technicians who, while well adapted to the bureaucratic techno-system of large communities, tend to be incapable of handling the more complex situations requiring a combination of technical and commercial skills. Not surprisingly, T. E. Clarke (1981) has found that

> 'businessmen from smaller high-technology companies had a greater dissatisfaction with university graduates than those from larger technology-based companies'.

The relevance of traditional academic education for entrepreneurship must be even more severely limited.

Innovation centres represent a useful addition to the battery of organisational mechanisms designed to facilitate technology transfer from universities to industry. It is important, however, that they do not become transformed into isolated activities carried out by a few enthusiasts at the periphery of a university.

A link to an applied research institute or a research park is probably necessary for successful long-term development of an innovation centre. Such a link will give the centres the necessary access to material and intellectual resources necessary for successful technical work and an additional contact surface with the business community.

Entrepreneurial culture

Entrepreneurship is more than a constellation of skills or an individual aptitude. It is a way of life, a culture. It thrives in some groups, and is almost wholly absent in others. Many academic communities, particularly in Europe, have traditionally belonged to the second category and cannot be changed without transforming the academic monoculture into a more pluralistic one. This transformation cannot be achieved without an organised effort to promote interactions between the academic community and the entrepreneurial segment of the business community.

The MIT's Enterprise Forum is one such example. It can be described as a highly informal organisation started by a group of MIT alumni with the aim of helping newly started companies. An interested entrepreneur or a firm can have its business/innovation problems discussed by an assembly of persons possessing relevant knowledge and experience. The Forum proceeds by setting up a panel of 5 — 10 experts who are expected to analyse and comment upon the client's problem. A workshop is then organised during which the entrepreneur/ company presents his/its problem before the panel and an invited audience. The ensuing discussions tend to be as informal as they are helpful. The innovator gets advice and feedback both from the specialised experts and from people with personal entrepreneurial experience. The academics, on the other hand, become familiar with the realities of the marketplace.

Organisations such as these while working in conjunction with science parks, innovation centres, liaison offices and the like have every chance of creating an important academic subculture which could greatly enhance the creativeness of universities.

The behaviour of the local business communities is also important in this context. The role of business surrounding a university does not have to be limited to provision of the markets and finance to the fledgling university-spun companies. Equally important could be the social interactions through which entrepreneurial lore could penetrate into the academic world.

References

Blumenthal, David A. 'Lifeforms, Computer Programs and the Pursuit of a Patent'. *Technology Review,* February/March 1983, pp.26 — 34

Clarke, T. E. 'Educating Technical Entrepreneurs and Innovators for the 1980s'. *Technovation,* 1, 1981

Colton, R. M. *'National Science Foundation Experience with University-Industry Centers for Scientific Research and Technological Innovation* (an analysis of issues, characteristics and criteria for their establishment)', Technovation 1, 1981

Colton, R. M. and Udell, G. 'The National Science Foundation's Innovation Centres — An Experiment in Training Potential Entrepreneurs and Innovators'. *Journal of Small Business Management,* Vol. 14, No. 2, 1976, pp. 11 — 20

Culliton, Barbara 'Harvard and Monsanto: the $23m. Alliance', *Science,* 25 February 1977. 'The Academic-Industrial Complex', *Science,* Vol. 216, 28 May 1982. 'Academe and Industry Debate Partnership', *Science,* Vol. 219, 14 January 1983, pp.150 — 151

Langrish, J. 'The Changing Relationship between Science and Technology', *Nature,* 250, August 1974

Layton, E. T. 'Conditions of Technological Development', *Science Technology and Society,* ed. Spiegel-Rosing and Price. London/Beverly Hills, Sage, 1977

Marver, J. D. and Patton, C. V., *The Correlates of Consultation: American Academics in the Real World,* Higher Education, 5 (1976), 319 — 335

Meyer-Thurow, Georg 'The Industrialisation of Invention: a case study from the German Chemical Industry', *ISIS,* Vol. 73, No. 268, 1972, pp. 363 — 381

Norman, Colin 'Electronic Firms Plug into the Universities', *Science,* Vol. 217, 6 August 1982

National Science Foundation (NSF), *Support of Basic Research by Industry.* Industrial Research Institute Corporation Study. August 1978 (NSF C76-21517)

National Science Foundation (NSF), University-Industry Research Relations, Fourteenth Annual Report of the National Science Board, Washington, 1982

OECD *The Research System.* 2 Vols. Committee for Scientific and Technological Policy. Paris 1972

OECD *Technical Change and Economic Policy* Paris 1980

Price, Derek J. de Solla *Is Technology Historically Independent of Science?* Symposium on the Historical Relations of Science and Technology (mimeo), Montreal, 1964.

Reimers, Niels 'Survey of Directed Mechanisms for Innovation of University Research'. *Les Nouvelles,* Vol. XV, No. 2, June 1980

Rothwell, R., (1982), *Evaluating the Effectiveness of Government Innovation Policy,* Six Countries Programme Report, Six Countries Secretariate, PO Box 215, TNO, 2600 AE Delft, The Netherlands, 1982

Shapero, Albert *University-Industry Interactions: Recurring Expectations, Unwarranted Assumptions and Feasible Policies.* Columbus, Ohio: Ohio State University, 31 July 1979

Sibru, M. A. et al. *The Formation of a Technology-Oriented Complex: Lessons from North America and European Experiences.* CPA Report 76 — 78. MIT Center for Policy Alternatives.

Universities and Industry Joint Committee, *Industry, Science and the Universities,* London, CBI, July 1970.

CHAPTER 6

Demand oriented instruments in innovation policy: government procurement and regulation

G. Houttuin

Procurement is a major mode of government influence on the process of innovation, but its effectiveness depends on the government's position – its relative dominance – in the market. Procurement, with its often enormous power to raise technical quality and competitive performance, is often used merely to buy as cheaply as possible. Prototype development and applied research is still an exception in most government procurement activity. Mr. Houttuin analyses the issues involved and notes some recent developments in several countries.

Mr. Guus Houttuin is Policy Adviser in the Technology Policy Division of the Dutch Ministry of Economic Affairs. He is involved in the conduct of bilateral cooperation programmes and in the evaluation of other countries' innovation policies. He holds a Masters degree in International Law from the University of Amsterdam.

Government is inevitably one of the major actors in the industrial innovation process: it is deeply involved in creating the framework in which industry operates as well as being a customer in large parts of the market.

This chapter will deal with government and its agencies in the latter capacity and will focus mainly on the effects on innovation brought about by government demand. As a consequence the procurement part of this chapter will be the largest whereas on regulation and its effects on innovation only a few introductory remarks will be made.

Introduction

A study by SPRU and TNO (1977) concluded that '...the most important way that governments have influenced technical innovation is through demand.' Government procurement concerns technology in various stages of research and development and under different market structures.

Objectives

The objectives of an innovation oriented procurement policy can be divided into three broad categories:

- Improving the quality of goods used in the public sector;
- Improving the quality of goods used in the private sector;
- Improving industry's competitiveness.

Improving the quality of public sector goods or achieving an optimal cost-benefit relationship is the primary objective of almost all procurement. It is important to make the distinction between the short term and long term cost-benefit balance. Short-term objectives are mainly a comparison of goods off-the-shelf, generally the chief task of the central procurement agencies. Longer term efficiency becomes an objective when government takes on the extra responsibility of industrial innovation and tries explicitly to influence prior stages of the innovation process and to raise technical know-how. Procedures typically used are the setting of performance specifications and value incentive clauses.

The second objective of innovation oriented procurement policy is to improve the quality of goods in the private sector, mainly where market conditions are imperfect, such as in energy conservation.

The third category lies in promoting the international competitiveness of industry and stems from traditional industrial policy. In the short term it is clear that most governments are under pressure from business, labour unions and members of parliament to use procurement to save or to create jobs. A much more interesting objective, and that is what this chapter is about, is to use procurement for the longer term competitiveness of industry.

There are some limitations on the use of procurement as an instrument for innovation policy. First of all, there may be a lack of consensus within government, resulting in frequent policy changes. This increases the uncertainty to firms and makes successful innovation unlikely.

A second limitation is the absence of market power on the side of government, especially when it is just one buyer among many. A third factor is the absence of competition between producers. This applies mainly to the smaller countries and markets. A fourth limitation of procurement policy is that government is not always capable of rational and long term decision making.

Stages of technological development

In the process of innovation a number of stages can be identified: applied research; feasibility studies; prototype development; diffusion and maturity (a mix of innovation and product life cycle). This scheme serves a number of objectives. First of all it is a chronological ordering. Most innovations can be presented along these lines. Secondly the stages correspond to recognisably different types of activities in the management of technology, be it in industry or in government. For example, applied research corresponds to the management problem of project selection in the research laboratories of large industrial firms and to the contracting out of research by a government department. Diffusion corresponds to a firm's possible second-in-the-market strategy or the government's efforts to promote technology transfer. The stage of maturity corresponds to the buying of goods off-the-shelf by procurement officers. Comparable projects at the early stages of development carry a much lower price tag than those at later stages. As a consequence in these early stages the possibilities of risk taking, parallel projects and competition among suppliers are much greater.

Thirdly this graduation reflects a scale of (decreasing) uncertainty for the decision makers involved in funding a procurement process and concurrently an increasing degree of possible demand specification. The concept of demand specification is explained by Eric Haeffner for the construction industry:

Specification Degree	Description
1	Technical R & D is needed
2	Technical R & D in an indicated field should be stimulated
3	Less costly and technically improved building materials are needed
4	Building materials for indicated use should be developed
5	Existing product with one or two improvements mentioned
6	The need for a new, not existing, product for specific use
7	Specific new product with one or several technical demands mentioned
8	Specific new product with complete specifications in figures are given.

Roughly similar stages can be recognised in most other technologies as well. He argues that as the process of innovation goes from stage one (technical R & D is needed) to stage eight (specific new product with complete specification) the degree of specification is gradually increased from very low to very high. And when government uses procurement to stimulate innovation, the degree of demand specification has great influence on the type of activities that can successfully be pursued by a given government organisation. Relatively little in-house competence is required for procurement activities at Haeffner's stage eight of technological development: it corresponds to buying goods off-the-shelf. No attempt is made to encourage the supplier to be innovative in any way other than by producing at the lowest possible cost (which may have an effect on the stimulation of advanced production systems).

Most government procurement falls within this category and specialised central buying agencies have usually been set up to maximise the price effect by ordering in large numbers.

It is only under the pressure of special circumstances that the buyer will accept more than a minimal uncertainty. Likewise, the manufacturer will respond only if some extra compensation is offered. The difficulties — and the chances of failure — increase as the degree of demand specification is lower. For this reason the general process of government procurement concerns itself mostly with buying off-the-shelf and much less frequently with diffusion or transfer of technology, even if proven elsewhere. In the procurement activities of government prototype development feasibility studies and applied research are still exceptions to the general rule of buying as cheaply as possible. Using general procurement to influence the prior stages of the innovation process requires a willingness to run larger risks and, usually, to spend larger amounts of money.

Apart from general procurement (with possible innovative consequences) there are in most countries specific procurement activities, based to a large extent on the government's science and technology policy. These activities tend to concentrate in the stages of technical development in which the degree of demand specification is low and the uncertainty with respect to successful application is high. Typical of this approach are the procurement of prototypes or demonstration projects. These procurement activities may often be functioning as a 'technology push', neglecting some elements of the necessary 'demand pull'.

Market structures

The government's market position — the extent to which it is the dominant buyer — is of primary importance to its influence on a market and therefore to its ability to promote innovation by means of an innovation oriented procurement policy.

It seems useful to make a distinction between monopsony, oligopsony and polyopsony to describe the market structure on the demand (procurement) side.

In the case of monopsony the government is the sole buyer in a market (segment). This is generally the case with military, space and — in some countries — telecommunications technology. It is clear that the potential for an innovation oriented procurement policy is greatest in the case of monopsony. However, the risk increases with the potential.

In the case of oligopsony a number of other large buyers are in the market, from the public or the private sector. In the Netherlands such a situation exists in low cost housing, where government as well as large corporations operate on the demand side. It is interesting to note that, analogous to the behaviour of the 'price leader' in the theory of oligopoly, one of the oligopsonists can play the role of 'quality leader'. It is also clear that within the framework of an oligopsonistic market it is quite possible to reach a co-operative relationship between purchasers and suppliers. This is of special importance to the latter group because of the uncertainties in innovation. One way is by means of an agreement between purchaser and supplier to buy only goods to specific standards in the future.

Polyopsony is the government's usual market position. Under such conditions the government can still attempt to pursue an active procurement policy aimed at innovation. But the effect will in principle be proportional to its share of the market and the effects on innovation may be equally limited. It is difficult for the government to 'guarantee' a sufficient market size for innovative products under oligopsonistic conditions; with polyopsony this becomes an even greater problem. The government should take care not to overestimate its influence nor to suggest to the manufacturer a larger market for products still to be developed than actually exists or will exist.

It seems preferable in the case of polyopsony to support an innovation oriented procurement policy in conjunction with other government measures such as regulation, prescribed labelling or well advertised demonstrations. In many cases the use of such instruments will require procurement activities in the early stages of technological development.

The market structure on the supply side also limits the scope of a procurement policy. A number of problems can be listed. First there is the situation of monopoly. If there is only one supplier there is a considerable danger of an incestuous relationship between him and the government, resulting in a lack of competitive pressure on technological performance. Since the government often does not have the freedom of the private firm to purchase abroad, competition becomes more difficult according as the economies of scale are greater or the country smaller.

Oligopoly also poses special problems. Some countries have creatively used this market structure by forcing parallel and competitive development or different technological approaches to a certain problem. Usually the government cannot allow any of the oligopolists to lose out completely.

A situation in which the market power of the suppliers is not sufficient for adequate profitability to finance R & D and other innovative activities can also be a serious obstacle to innovative procurement.

Recent initiatives

The Netherlands. In April 1981 a white paper on procurement policy and innovation *(Aanschaffingsbeleid en Innovatie)* was presented to Parliament. According to this paper substantial government demand can be used to stimulate innovation in industry (demand pull) or government itself may need innovative products or services (technology push). Part of the paper consists of proposals for better coordination of government procurement e.g. by the establishment of a central procurement coordinating division directly under the Minister of Economic Affairs. Within this Department a budget of 20 million DFl (1981) has been earmarked for special inter-departmental projects. The Ministry partly finances new development work in industry that is directly related to specific government procurement projects. Reference is also made to the stimulating role government laboratories can play and to the need for improved collaboration between the procurement agencies, the research institutions and industry.

An example of an innovative procurement project according to the ideas put forward in the paper is an office automation project ('Docsyst') in the Ministries of the Interior, Housing, and Finance. These Ministries each contributed to the hardware side of the project while the Ministry of Economic Affairs and Philips paid for the development of the necessary software. Although it is too early to make an evaluation of Dutch innovative procurement policy there is no doubt that government has had some success in shifting from short-term policy objectives to medium and long-term objectives, i.e. the stimulation of innovation.

This change of attitude can probably best be illustrated by the recently published information technology plan (*Informatica Stimulerings Plan,* 1984) which proposes some interesting measures against the following background: Government is one of the largest information-processors in the Netherlands with an annual budget of some 1.5 billion guilders. The information technology market (IT market) has an annual growth rate of 10%.

With this market position government has the greatest opportunities for the stimulation of innovation. Mentioned are a coordinated procurement policy, the contracting out of development work and privatisation. Some of the measures envisaged are:

— a more direct involvement of industry in the definition phase of IT projects within government, especially in the development of IT systems and software;
— Together with industry a limited number of advanced IT projects will be chosen, with the following objectives: to improve the efficiency and quality of government services, to promote better cooperation between government and research establishments and to increase industrial competitiveness.

United Kingdom. The Department of Trade and Industry has a scheme by which it can purchase a certain number of pre-production models of new or significantly improved equipment which the manufacturer is having difficulty launching. The equipment is placed with potential users (mainly within government or nationalised industries) to test and evaluate before they decide whether to purchase or not. This scheme has now been enlarged to include not only individual products but also complete systems. The best example is the office automation strategy of the Department of Trade and Industry, which serves not only to stimulate innovation with the manufacturer concerned but also as a pilot and demonstration project.

For the user these projects are a way of comparing different systems, and also a route to unbiased practical experience in working with office automation. For the industry, they provide a realistic proving ground for advanced technology, and an endorsement of the public sector's belief in automation. The basic idea is for the Department to select different types of users and then match their requirements with an appropriately designed office automation system. User and manufacturer would feed back information on operating experience at intervals over the trial period, and at the end of the whole exercise all the findings would be published. If the system has been operating satisfactorily the user can purchase the system already at its disposal at a special price. There are at present 20 'Offices of the Future' running in working units of public sector organisations.

Another interesting development was the publication by the Advisory Council for Applied Research and Development of a report on R & D for Public Purchasing (February 1980). A working group examined R & D relationships between purchasers and suppliers in five industries where the public sector dominates the U.K. market for goods or services. These industries were: coal mining machinery, rail transport, road construction, water supply and treatment, and gas supply and distribution. It was concluded that in general too much R & D is carried out by the public sector in support of its purchasing decisions. Moreover the R & D programmes of public sector purchasing organisations do not explicitly take the needs of suppliers into account, but are aimed solely at meeting the requirements of the organisation.

The technical competitiveness of U.K. industry in export markets would be enhanced if public sector purchasing organisations — which account for about half of the applied R & D carried out in the U.K. — relied more on their suppliers' own R & D or contracted out more of their R & D requirements to the private sector. In particular, R & D that should lead to products or expertise marketable outside the U.K. public sector is the proper responsibility of the supplier, although financial support from the purchaser may be desirable. Where a programme of work supported by the public sector is capable of leading within five years to equipment or expertise which can be marketed outside the U.K. public sector, there should be private sector participation in planning, direction and funding of work. According to the report, however, a sudden transfer of R & D to the private sector would not be wise. Many firms have become accustomed to relying on the public sector's in house R & D to define the technical characteristics of the products required and will need to adjust to undertaking more R & D themselves.

Ireland. A number of measures have been introduced over the years aimed at stimulating innovation, though none can be regarded as demand oriented. The government is aware of the need to create a suitable climate of opinion for the acceptance and integration of the quality assurance ethic into the business life of the country. This will require a long term promotion programme of national dimensions to educate industry as to the need for quality. For its procurement policy the government is considering the use of quality standards before awarding government contracts to firms. Irish Standards on quality systems will be sealed by the government later in 1984. A programme to improve the level of quality awareness in Irish industry will be launched after the publication of the quality system standards. The programme's first phase will be the implementation of a five year Quality Awareness Plan which will set out definite measurable targets to be achieved in the lifetime of the plan. Government procurement policy will play a major role in implementing the plan. It is envisaged that various government departments will over a number of years purchase products only from companies that are certified as having implemented quality standards. Thus the use of quality standards will assist companies in obtaining government contracts, and also in obtaining a larger share of the sub-supply market and improve the company's competitiveness.

The above measures, which are still in the planning phase, can equally fall under the heading of government regulation.

Belgium. In Belgium a Ministerial Committee has been established for the direction and orientation of public procurement ('Commissie voor orientatie en coordinatie van de overheidsopdrachten'). The Committee prepares an annual plan for the multi-annual procurement programmes (rolling plan) so as to enhance technological and scientific research and to stimulate industrial cooperation.

As to the objectives of Government procurement policy there is an interesting chapter on government investment in a publication by the Ministry of Economic Affairs on a new industrial policy: Public investment is to be a natural follow-up to scientific research: public needs such as transport, energy, telecommunications, defence and health have a significant potential for stimulating technological growth. The link between government financed R & D in the above sectors and the application of the R & D results should naturally lead to the government buying its 'own' product. Buying a product originating in government subsidised R & D will in the future be considered as the last and necessary phase of R & D support.

Especially for smaller countries public procurement is often the only way to provide an industrial reference (first sale or industrial application) to new products or techniques. This reference then has to open markets. The last statement raises some doubts. As mentioned in the paragraph on objectives, government should not overestimate its market power and, especially in the European community, the smaller countries should always look for export possibilities.

Canada. In 1972, the government established a contracting-out policy which directs that government requirements for mission-oriented science and technology are to be contracted out to the private sector, preferably to Canadian industry, unless a department can justify intramural or foreign performance. The policy applies to present and new requirements in all scientific activities in the natural sciences and to human science requirements in the fields of urban, regional and transportation studies. Although the contracting out policy is primarily a procurement policy, it is intended to promote the development of a Canadian industrial R & D capability. It is expected that $275 million of government science requirements will be contracted out in 1983/84.

In 1974, the government expanded the contracting out policy to cover *unsolicited* science and technology *proposals* which are submitted by industry and which fall within the remit of a government department. The UP Programme is intended to permit the government to respond quickly to sound, unique proposals from the private sector in support of government science missions.

The Department of Supply and Services administers a fund which provides bridge financing for proposals which are accepted from the point of view of sponsorship, scientific merit and uniqueness, but which cannot be funded from the sponsoring department's current appropria-tions.

In 1981 the Source Development Fund (SDF) was established to allow the government to make better use of procurement as an industrial development tool. The SDF was designed as an adjunct to the procurement review mechanism to help develop a 'source' as a supplier for government when a broader market exists by means of which Canada could derive significant economic benefit from this investment. The SDF pays for the incremental costs of high technology procurement-related developments which need up-front funding. The fund also supports product innovation and maximisation of Canadian content.

The Profit Policy directive sets out the policy and guidelines for the calculation of the profit applicable to negotiated contracts with the Canadian suppliers for both products and services to special specifications with total costs of $1 million or over. The amount of profit to be applied will be calculated on the basis of four factors: capital employed, general business risk, contractual risk, and contractor's contribution to a Canadian Value Added Strategy. Promotion of R & D in Canada is one of the areas in which recognition of the Canadian Value Added will be made for profit purposes.

Sweden. The National Swedish Board for Technical Development (Styrelsen for Teknisk Utveckling, STU) is the agency which organises and implements industrial and techno-logy policy for the Department of Industry.

Since 1978 STU has provided a service to help public authorities in their technology procurement, especially when an authority needs goods or services not yet on the market, and which would need specific development work to meet the specifications. The main customers for the STU service are the 25 county councils and 270 local authorities. A particularly important aspect of STU's support is when several agencies coordinate their new technology requirements. Because of the autonomy of local authorities, such coordination is voluntary and usually arranged through either the Swedish Association of Local Authorities or the County Councils Association. STU financially supports:

— procurement agencies' feasibility studies and writing specifications for new technology;
— development work which is included in the procurement contract.

Examples of technology procurement priority areas are:

— handling and disposal of household waste;
— data processing systems for local authority technical departments like energy supply, roads, public building, and water and sewage treatment;
— fire and rescue services technology;
— traffic control systems for public transport.

In the 1983 STU Forward Look, which covers the period

July 1984 — June 1987 there is a change in emphasis. In the past the main worries about technology procurement concerned the public sector. Now the emphasis has switched to transfer between companies in the private sector. The 'new' function of STU is to improve the conditions for technology transfer as an effective way of maximising the benefit to both seller and purchaser of development work. Finance may be needed to develop the contractual background and the specifications for new technology. There are three classes of circumstances: when the buyer takes the initiative help is offered with the technical evaluation and the planning of the negotiations; when the seller of an existing technology decides to offer an improvement; and thirdly when a developer for an idea is sought, where help is offered to promote links between the parties.

France. A recent French initiative is the TEP system ('transfer-evaluation-prototype'). It is somewhat similar to the pre-production model scheme of the United Kingdom. The main difference lies in the fact that cross-fertilisation between technologies and/or technology applications is stimulated. For example the military application of laser technology is used in the field of medical technology.

Conclusions

Innovation oriented procurement policy, however difficult to implement, is still an important part of innovation policy.

There is a slight tendency to incorporate innovative procurement in other science and technology policy instruments such as the information technology plans in the United Kingdom and the Netherlands. This trend could result in procurement policy losing some of its value-for-money characteristics, which is a good thing.

Some remarks on government regulation

As this chapter deals with demand oriented instruments in innovation policy, government regulation falls only to a limited extent within its scope.

The demand-aspect of government regulation is only one of many (e.g. public health, safety, value for money).

Government regulation is generally considered an impediment to innovation rather than as a stimulus to it and most studies focus on its possible negative impact. This is hardly surprising, bearing in mind the pace of technological innovation and the slow response to these changes by overbureaucratic government agencies.

Even 'positive' government action in the field of regulation is seen as serving only to limit the possible negative consequences of regulation. This is sometimes too harsh. A good example is the use of performance standards instead of requirement standards, a practice which has steadily gained ground.

Deregulation

In the wake of privatisation (e.g. in the United States and the United Kingdom) deregulation has become an important policy issue. In the Netherlands, deregulation policy was a response to complaints from industry about the negative impact of regulation on industrial and technological development.

Deregulation, at least for the Netherlands, does not mean that all government regulations which may have a negative impact on innovation will be abolished. It means reducing the number of regulations but also reformulating and simplifying them. Of several deregulation projects started at the beginning of 1983, some have still not been implemented due to stubborn resistance on the part of various social groups, not to mention civil servants.

CHAPTER 7

Evaluation of Innovation Policy

Dr. R. Rothwell

Dr. Roy Rothwell has been a frequent participant at Six Countries Workshops and has published several books in collaboration with Professor W. Zegveld, based at least in part on presentations at Workshops. He prepared the report on evaluation and innovation policy following a Workshop on this subject in December. He stresses again the crucial importance of employing multiple indicators in evaluating effectiveness. The elements of the policy system are highly interdependent and interactive and problems of measurement are inherent in the nature of the system. Those involved in policy evaluation should be concerned with seeking convergence between different indicators rather than relying on judgements derived from any single one.

A physicist, Dr. Rothwell worked first in research and development in telecommunications and later joined the Science Policy Research Unit, University of Sussex, where he is now a Senior Fellow. He is perhaps best known for his work on the SAPPHO Project, the major study on the factors associated with success and failure in industrial innovation. He has followed this with studies of innovation in small firms and in the textile machinery and agricultural engineering industries. He has written several books, some in conjunction with Walter Zegveld, a founder of the Six Countries Programme.

Introduction

Innovation policy instruments and the philosophies underlying their use vary considerably from country to country. While some policy instruments have been employed for many years, for example R and D credits and collective industrial research institutes, other instruments have only more recently been employed as explicit tools of innovation policy, for example innovation oriented procurement (Rothwell and Zegveld, 1981; Overmeer and Prakke, 1979). Even those instruments that have a relatively long history of use in attempting to stimulate industrial innovations, however, have rarely been subjected to systematic and objective evaluation concerning their effectiveness, although there has been a considerable number of surveys undertaken of industrial innovations including the impact of public policies (Piatier, 1983). Because of this, innovation policy as practised today might generally be said to be more an object of faith rather than understanding.

There have, of course, been a number of exceptions to this rule, perhaps the most notable being the Experimental Technology Incentives Programme (ETIP) of the U.S. Department of Commerce. ETIP consisted of a series of explicit innovation policy experiments, each of which was subjected to careful and objective evaluation (Herbert and Hoar, 1982). More recently in Europe a number of innovation policy initiatives have also been systematically evaluated (DTI, 1982; ISI (Meyer-Krahmer et al.), 1983). Given the current pressures on government in a large number of countries to curb public expenditures, it seems likely that a major requirement of any new public policy initiative will be 'demonstration of effectiveness'. In other words, public policies, and the institutions involved in their implementation, increasingly will be called upon to demonstrate 'value for money'. This is evident, for example, in the case of the Alvey Programme in the U.K., which is a major national programme for the creation of an internationally competitive information technology industry. An important feature of the Alvey Programme is that it will be subjected to continuous and systematic evaluation by teams not involved in its implementation (Rothwell and Zegveld, 1985).

Despite the general paucity of systematic policy evaluations, it nevertheless is possible to identify a number of the principal difficulties innovation policies have in the past suffered from:

(i) a lack of market know-how amongst public policy makers. According to Golding (1978) and Little (1974) there exists evidence to suggest that government funds often have gone to support projects of high technical sophistication but of low market potential and profitability. As well as often having lower market potential, projects funded by governments have also tended to involve higher technical and financial risks than those funded wholly by industrial companies. That government backed projects involve high technical risk might, of course, be taken as justification for government involvement in the first place; the problem governments face is to identify high-risk projects that also have high market potential, yet it is doubtful whether government policy-makers generally possess the competence to assess market prospects satisfactorily.

(ii) The fact that, in the past, subsidies have tended to assist mainly large firms, an imbalance that can and should be redressed. This tells us nothing, of course, about the effectiveness of those subsidies that have been made to small firms. In the case of large firms, evidence from Canada and the Federal Republic of Germany suggests that funds often have gone in support of projects that are relatively small and sometimes of dubious merit such that the companies would not, by themselves, finance them. The Enterprise Development Program in Canada, which will support only projects that represent a significant risk to the firm, represents an explicit attempt to avoid financing marginal projects in large firms.

(iii) Governments have tended to adopt a passive, rather than an active, stance towards information dissemination. As a result, policy measures have been taken up largely by a limited number of 'aware' (usually large) companies.

(iv) The lack of practical knowledge, or imaginative conceptualisation, of the process of industrial innovation by policy-makers. As a result, they have tended to adopt an R & D oriented view of innovation, often to the detriment of other important aspects of the process, e.g. innovation- oriented public purchasing.

(v) The lack of interdepartmental coordination — and sometimes cooperation — between the relevant organisations and agencies involved in the policy process. This can result in lack of complementarity between different initiatives, and might also lead to the propagation of contradictory measures.

(vi) A tendency for innovation policies to be subjected to changes in political philosophy rather than to changing national or international economic needs or conditions.

The Policy System

In his overview paper presented at the Six Countries Workshop on Evaluating the Effectiveness of Innovation Policies, Gibbons (1982) states:

> 'Firstly, the range of policies is extremely large and, as formulated, are seldom directed at a single objective or even at a single government department. In other words, government innovation policies involve multiple actors. To some extent this is a feature of a good deal of government policy but the effects are more difficult to handle in the case of innovation policy because these policies involve as an intrinsic element non-governmental organisations, mainly firms, trade unions and banks.'

The implications of the above are that any meaningful assessment of the effectiveness of government innovation policies should be carried out in the context of the overall policy system and should take account of the dominant actors involved at the different stages of policy formulation and implementation. At the simplest level we might represent the public policy process as in Figure 1 and this, straight away, suggests a useful definition of policy evaluation:

'Policy evaluation is concerned with measuring the degree to which public policy initiatives succeed in achieving their stated aims — as well as with evaluating the assumptions underlying the policies and identifiying non-intended effects.'

FIGURE 1
Public Policy: Goals, Means, Satisfaction

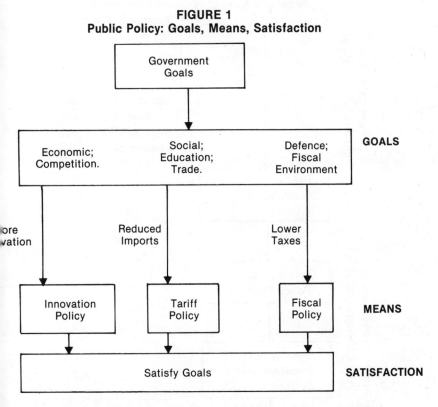

Assessment = Measuring the degree to which goals are satisfied.

Figure 1 also illustrates that:

— Innovation is only one of a wide set of policies available to government in attaining various goals.
— There is a high degree of interdependence between goals.

— There are common elements between policies as well as many elements within each policy area.

FIGURE 2
The Policy Formulation and Implementation Process

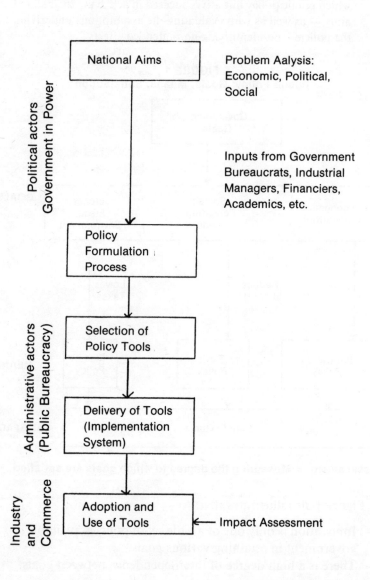

We are thus dealing with a highly interdependent and interactive *system* and separating the various influences acting within this system might be difficult. We can, therefore, see at the outset that *there may be severe problems* of measurement as a consequence of the nature of the policy system *itself*. Further, in terms of policy effectiveness, tackling just one part of the system might not be sufficient, and constraints elsewhere might neutralise the positive influences of a particular initiative. Those involved in policy evaluation should be made explicitly aware of such possibilities from the start (see Chapters 2 and 3).

Figure 2 offers a simple schema of the policy formulation and implementation process. The point of presenting this schema is to emphasise that the assessment of policy effectiveness has something to do with *all* five phases. In the first case, if the original analysis of national problems is wrong, then we might not expect a favourable outcome from subsequent initiatives based on this analysis. Second, given the establishment of appropriate aims, there is then the problem of formulating appropriate policies and of selecting appropriate tools. This will generally involve many actors who might represent different — and sometimes conflicting — interests, and attaining a reasonable balance between them might be impossible. For example, if political dogma outweighs economic considerations, we might well see the wrong policies established and the wrong tools used. The point is, we should be aware of these possibilities when assessing particular policy tools: there might be little inherently wrong with the tool or its mode of use; it might simply be the wrong tool.

Next we need to investigate the delivery system. Such factors as bureaucracy, lack of dissemination, lack of regional representation, and unclear or inappropriate decision criteria, can all invalidate the use of an entirely appropriate tool based on solid policy analysis. Finally, managers' expectations of the costs and benefits associated with the use of a policy tool will be instrumental in determining its rate of take-up, and evaluation should be concerned with eliciting these perceptions and discovering the reasons underlying them.

To summarise, any evaluation of the effectiveness of a policy tool or group of tools should include consideration of the complete policy system and its *institutions*.

Policy Evaluation

After Nelson (1974), Gibbons (1982) has identified three analytical traditions in rational policy analysis. These are:

> (i) The allocation of resources to science and technology;
> (ii) The organisation and control of economic activity;
> (iii) Public policy analysis.

The first tradition views the problem as stemming from past allocation of scientific resources and proposes solutions in terms of the reallocation of R & D activities. Good examples are Farina and Gibbons' (1979) analysis of the Brvity and concentration, and Irvine and Martin's (1981) study of the effectiveness of the Norwegian system for the support of R & D activities in collective research laboratories. Important points to emerge from these studies were the importance of answering the question 'What *difference* did the policy initiative make?' rather than simply 'What happened?', and the crucial importance of employing *multiple* partial indicators and of seeking convergence between them.

The second tradition concerns itself primarily with *institutional structures* whose characteristics determine the way in which resources are allocated. The two main sets of emphasis within this tradition concern *demand* conditions ('what is worth what cost and what is better than what; and monitoring resource flows into the sector') and *supply* conditions ('evaluating the machinery that is supplying what is demanded').

The principal method utilised in demand side evaluation ('trying to evaluate what costs what') is cost-benefit analysis. An example of this is Gardiner's study of launching aid in the U.K. aircraft industry (Gardiner, 1975), which showed that the rate of return to public investment was small or nil, and which might be taken to indicate an ineffective allocation of resources or even, taking into account opportunity costs, a misallocation of resources. As Gibbons has pointed out, however, before making this judgement it is important to question whether the objective of the policy was to stimulate aero-engine development or to obtain a given return on public capital invested (Gibbons, 1982, *op. cit.*). Concerning supply side evaluation, Gibbons has offered Kogan et al.'s (1980) study of the commissioning of research in the Department of Health and Social Security (DHSS) as an illustrative example. This study showed how the organisational context, in which DHSS funded researchers and policy makers interact, clearly influenced the nature of that interaction.

Significant methodological implications of these studies are:

— Before any meaningful evaluation can be undertaken, the precise policy aims of the intervention must be established, e.g. in the case of an aircraft launching aid, was it designed primarily to produce a high return on public investment or to stimulate aircraft develop-ments?
— Public, as well as private rates of return to innovation policy-oriented public investment should, where possible, be included in any assessment of policy effectiveness. The former, however, might be highly diffuse and of longer-term perspective, and thus difficult to measure accurately or meaningfully.
— Policy assessment should, where the outcome is unfavourable, seek to discover the role played by institutions and their procedures in determining this outcome.

The third tradition promises a 'rational analysis to policy problems', which refers to

> 'the laying out of alternative courses of action, of tracing their consequences in terms of benefits and costs, and identifying a best or at least a "good" policy. The utility of such analysis was seen in terms of providing guidance for the policy maker so that he could choose more intelligently, from the range of alternatives presented, what needed to be done.'

According to Nelson (1974),

> '... the scriptures of the policy analysis tradition have been

marked by a shift of emphasis from before the fact analysis, to evaluation of programmes *ex post,* to deliberate experimental development of policy.'

Gibbons has explored a major example of a 'second phase' policy analysis, namely the comparative analysis by de Leon of the nuclear reactor programmes of six nations. The most significant methodological implication of de Leon's analysis is that it was conducted within an explicit framework of 'multiple actors, multiple objectives and different times'. For such major national programmes of technological development it is possible to suggest that (de Leon, 1976):

— Different organisations and their objectives are particularly crucial or even predominant at certain stages of the design and dissemination process.
— Different attributes are essential for the achievement of different objectives.
— Technology development programmes can be viewed as having multiple actors and objectives which means that a single evaluative standard for a technology development programme is inadequate and potentially misleading.
— Costs grow as development progresses and early uncertainties are resolved.

Adopting a somewhat different approach Hetman (1983), drawing on the experiences of a number of OECD member countries in policy evaluation, has constructed a schema which attempts, for *different elements* of innovation policy, to establish a set of *evaluation criteria* and a corresponding set of *evaluation methods.* His results are shown in Table 1. These results, and those of Gibbons, suggest that the appropriate evaluation technique will vary with the type of policy instrument adopted and with special policy aims.

Policy Evaluation: some critical issues

Below we shall outline some of the more specific issues that emerged from the 1982 Six Countries Workshop discussions regarding policy evaluation. Beforehand, however, it is worthwhile summarising a number of rather general points that governments intent on innovation policy evaluation should bear in mind:

1. Because of the high-risk, high uncertainty and interdependent nature of the industrial innovation process and of the actors involved, there are inherent limitations to what public innovation policies can achieve (Rothwell and Zegveld, 1985).

2. Industrial innovation is a high-risk undertaking and many projects inevitably will fail. Governments should be aware of this at the outset and be willing to accept the possibility — indeed the probability — of failure in companies taking up specific policy initiatives.

3. Because innovation is a dynamic process, the policy system should be sufficiently flexible and responsive to accommodate the possibility of rapid change. It should also be sufficiently flexible to accommodate different types of innovation produced in greatly differing contexts or, alternatively, be tailored to suit specific situations.

4. The highly interactive and interdependent nature of the policy system might itself impose certain limitations on the precision with which policy effectiveness can be measured.

5. Because of this interactive nature, evaluations should encompass as much of the policy system as is practicable, rather than focus solely on individual elements within that system.

6. Policies do not implement themselves; nor does general awareness occur spontaneously. Governments must therefore adopt a positive approach to the dissemination of information regarding new initiatives and be willing to allocate sufficient resources to this end.

TABLE 1.

Policy objectives, incentives, evaluation criteria and evaluation procedures.

I — Financing

Innovation policy objectives	Incentives	Evaluation criteria	Evaluation procedures
Innovation potential of the national economy	Tax incentives to R & D	Balance of payments; trade balance	Statistical analysis and expertise
Innovation capacity of industry	Tax incentives to investment; Selective credit policy	Technological balance (patents and licensing agreements). R & D expenditures R & D personnel	Statistical analysis and expertise; Surveys and statistical analysis
Firms' innovation capacity, especially that of small and medium sized enterprises	Support for R & D Aid in launching new products	Invention rate (new ideas) Innovation rate (technical development) Marketing (new products)	Surveys Interviews; Surveys Interviews; Surveys, Expertise Statistics
Innovation capacity of collective R & D institutes	Aid in exploiting R & D results	Development and marketing rate	Surveys Statistics Audits
New technologies and advanced technology industries	Financing of technology streams; Financing of crash programmes	Technology content (new products and processes) Economic performance (turnover/export ratio, licences taken out and granted)	Audits Surveys Statistics

II — Innovation Infrastructures

Development of technical culture	Technical education / Vocational training	Level of understanding of technological changes / Adaptability / Employment structure	Analysis of subject matter and content of school curricula / Interviews / Surveys / Statistics / Audits
Technical information and assistance	Innovation advisory services, Technico-commercial advisory services	Number, nature and quality of contacts and consultations	Interviews / Audits
Diffusion of newly acquired scientific know-how	University/industry relations	Diffusion channels / modes of cooperation / Exchanges of personnel	Expertise / Seminars / Symposia
Technology transfer	Relations between public R & D bodies and industry	Number and nature of findings passed on. / Modes of transfer	Surveys / Audits / Statistics

III — Conditions of Competition and Regulations

Protection of innovation Patents system	Reforms of patents system legislation on licensing	Number and nature of patentable innovations / Patents balance / Licences balance	Statistics / Expertise
Regulatory frameworks	Anti-trust legislation / Flexible application of regulations	Propensity to innovate relative to size of firm	Surveys / Statistics / Expertise
Procurement framework	Tendering procedures / Terms of payment	Propensity to innovate relative to size and nature of public contract	Statistics / Surveys / Audits and nature of public contract
Public-sector investment policy (government and public enterprises)	Financing priorities / Selective credit policy / Part payment of tax or social insurance charges	Development of R & D activities. Scale and nature of public sector spin-off	Surveys / Statistics / Audits

Source: Hetman, 1983

7. Evaluation is not a costless process and, if it is to be carried out successfully, might require the commitment of considerable resources. Governments must be willing to bear this cost; an inadequately performed evaluation can be as bad as no evaluation and even worse if the results are misleading.

8. With certain policy initiatives, e.g. major national R & D projects, both the institutions involved with, and the output from, the initiative might vary over time. As a consequence evaluation criteria must be formulated relevant to the different stages of the programme.

9. While the object of innovation policies is to change things for the better, it must be accepted that they can have the opposite effect. Large, prestigious lobby projects, that often lack market awareness might, for example, result in a misallocation of resources with the accompanying opportunity costs to other, more promising, areas. This re-emphasises the need, from the outset, to take a rather broad view during policy evaluation.

10. Policy evaluation should look not only at the outcome of the use of specific policy initiatives, but also at the institutions involved in policy formulation and implementation and their procedures, as well as the relationships between them (interagency coordination; interdepartmental rivalry, etc.). In other words, policy evaluation should be concerned not simply with the question 'What change occurred as a result of policy?', but also 'why?', and 'how?' that change occurred. It is necessary to understand the network of interactions within the policy system before potential synergies can be capitalised on and bottlenecks removed.

11. Governments should be honest at the outset (at least with themselves!) regarding the true objectives of an evaluation. Is it part of a legitimation process? Is it part of a process of budgetary cuts? Or is it an attempt

genuinely to understand policy effectiveness and why? The reason underlying the evaluation decision will largely determine the use made of the results and, in some countries, their dissemination. In the longer term, the cynical political use of policy evaluation will tend to discredit the policy system as a whole.

12. Emphasis should be placed on forging links between the different institutions and actors involved in the policy formulation and implementation process (increased interdepartmental coordination) and between these and the user. While the user (industry) should clearly have a say in the policy formulation process, it should be recognised that managers often take a short-term view whereas policymakers often wish to look much further into the future. In the case of measures designed to induce changes in the shorter-term, industry might have a major say and be regarded as the primary customer. For long-term measures designed to induce fundamental structural changes in industry, government must play the dominant role and be regarded as the primary customer.

13. In order to accommodate radical innovations, companies often need to adopt novel organisational forms, e.g. the new ventures initiatives. For its proper implementation, innovation policy might similarly require the adoption of novel institutional forms. In other words current institutions within the public administration, and those involved directly in implementation (e.g. government R & D labs), might need to adapt themselves to suit better the requirements of innovation policy, rather than vice versa. Traditional institutional structures and attitudes might impose limitations on the kinds of innovation policy the system can accommodate.

Policy aims

Before any attempt can be made to evaluate the effectiveness of an innovation policy initiative, a clear statement must be made describing, unequivocally, the policy aims the initiative is designed to satisfy. If policy statements are 'fuzzy' regarding aims, any assessment inevitably will be a great deal 'fuzzier'. Where no primary aims are stated explicitly at the outset, the initiative might be justified on the basis of secondary or even tertiary effects which, clearly, would be misleading.

The Evaluators

A crucial issue is that of *who* performs the evaluation, and a number of suggestions were made on this point: government agencies, industry, academics, the institution under assessment, professional evaluation groups. A strong theme during the Workshop was that evaluation should not be left solely in the hands of those involved in policy formulation and implementation, because of potential problems of subjectivity in measurment and in inter-pretation.

If public bureaucracies are to be involved they might, to gain *objectivity* in measurement and *credibility* with the user, either:

— create a central, autonomous staff function devoted to evaluation, as per the private sector, or
— create a central staff function to allocate evaluation to outside agencies and to monitor their progress.

In the case of industry, while managers should clearly have a say in evaluation, it must be recognised that they also can be highly subjective in their judgements. In the case, for example, of R & D credits, it is not inconceivable that managers would overestimate the benefit in order to ensure future cash support. Managers might also — especially in companies or industries with no strong traditions of innovativeness — emphasise the value of short-term measures to the detriment of those designed to induce longer-term changes. Finally, while managers might recognise the benefits accruing from the use of *direct* tools, they might fail to capture in their assessment the benefits from *indirect,* or environmental measures, e.g. inputs from the scientific and technological infrastructure.

The best favoured solution was seen to be the use of an entirely independent body of assessors, be they academics or professional consultancy groups. Or, perhaps, as Coleman (1972) has suggested, more than one group should be used, especially for major and/or politically sensitive evaluations.

It is also essential to address the question of the range of skills contained within the evaluator group. They should have expertise in the particular field under investigation (industrial, techno/economic, organisational) as well as expertise in the *process of evaluation.* The appropriate mix of skills will, of course, vary from project to project.

Manifestations of Change

If the purpose of evaluation is to measure the changes induced by a particular policy initiative, then it is clearly necessary to determine those measurable factors that indicate the degree of change. If, for example, a measure is designed to increase the overall innovativeness of firms in a sector, or firms in a certain size category, or whatever, is it possible meaningfully to measure increased rates of innovation? Can this be measured directly? Does a figure for the current (pre-policy) innovation rate exist? Or is it necessary to measure innovation rates indirectly via, for example, R & D expenditures or patenting activity?

With specific or directed tools, measurement generally will be rather more straightforward than with environmental measures. It might, for example, be relatively straightforward to measure changes in R & D expenditure as a result of a scheme offering R & D credits; it would be more difficult to chart the effects of a reduction in corporation tax as an incentive to increased R & D and productivity related expenditures, since they will be generally more diffuse. The problem of establishing causality is correspondingly greater. Even in the former case, firms might use the measure at least partially to reduce their future R & D costs. This means, of course, that ideally measurement should contain a strong element of *comparison;* the existence of a *control group* will greatly enhance the meaningfulness of the measurements.

There is then the question of measuring qualitative changes. As we have discussed, there are many problems in seeking solely the perceptions of managers as an index of effectiveness. Nevertheless, management perceptions are not unimportant, especially where quantification of policy impacts is difficult. This leads us back to the crucial point made earlier that *multiple indicators* of effectiveness should be sought, and that evaluation should be concerned with seeking *convergence* between these different indicators; between the opinions of different groups and between different quantitative measures or proxies where these exist.

One rather crucial qualitative change is *company culture.* In any evaluation it is important to ask the question, even in the absence of any measurable short-term quantitative indication of change within the firm, 'Has government policy changed the culture of the firm?' In the longer-term, changes in management attitude towards innovation will be of much greater significance than, say, take-up by the firm today of R & D credits. Without such cultural changes the firm, when R & D credits are discontinued, is likely to move back to its original (lower) level of R & D expenditure.

This leads to the question of the use of the various indicators as a measure of policy success, which implies the need, in the first place, for success criteria. In general, *given that the tool* is appropriate to meeting policy *aims,* success should take into account at least the following:

— utility from the point of view of actual users (effectiveness of the tool in use);
— diffusion of use amongst the population of potential users (take-up rate);
— representativeness of use among different classes of potential users (e.g. large or small firms);
— positive attitudinal changes induced in firms through take-up.

We turn now to the question of precision of measurement and completeness of data. It was felt overwhelmingly at the 1982 workshop that, for the purpose of policy evaluation, great precision of measurement was not necessary and might in many instances be meaningless. Approximate results, complete enough to demonstrate causality, are sufficient. In terms of technique, the message was unequivocally 'keep it simple': evaluators should adopt a policy of 'satisficing'; providing 'good enough' data at the right time. In short, evaluation is the 'art of the possible'.

Timing of Evaluation

As implied above, the timing of an evaluation scheme is a crucial factor in determining its success. There are two aspects to this: in the first case there is the question of how long it does, or it should, take a particular initiative to have a significant and measurable impact; in the second case, and related to the first, if we wish to use the evaluation as a means of improving the initiative — i.e. establish a positive feedback loop — then how soon can this be achieved? From the point of view of improving the policy tool, probably the sooner the better. It was also pointed out that evaluations take time and governments should not be in too much of a hurry to generate results; hurried results are likely to be poor results.

Explaining the Outcome

One use of the results of a policy evaluation is simply to determine whether or not the policy initiative should continue. It was, however, felt strongly at the 1982 Workshop that policy evaluation should go further; that it should become a tool positively for improving the policy system. To achieve this, of course, the evaluation would have to answer not just the question 'What happened as a result of the policy initiative?', but also the question 'Why did this happen?'. This would involve looking at policy formulation, implementation and utilisation:

— was the original analysis of the problem correct?
— were the policy tools adopted appropriate to the solution of this problem?
— was the implementation system adequate?
— were the tools appropriately used in adopter companies?
— if not, was this due to poor selection procedures or an inadequate system of monitoring?
— did changing circumstances invalidate the original analysis?
— why did some companies reject the use of the tool? ... and so on ...

Establishing Feedback

An oft repeated theme of the Workshop was that the evaluation process — yielding 'what happened' and 'why' — should become an integral part of the policy system. Built-in feedback from evaluation would result in a flexible and responsive policy system undergoing continuous adjustment and improvement. The achievement of this, however, would require commitment, on the part of those involved in both policy formulation and delivery, to the implementation of the results of evaluation. Because of strong lobbies and other entrenched interests, this might not easily be forthcoming. Whatever evaluation scheme is adopted must therefore be credible to all those involved in the policy system.

With built-in feedback timing would, of course, be crucial, as would the ability to identify points of maximum leverage within the policy system in order to achieve *maximum change* at *minimum effort* and *at the appropriate time.* As an aid to both analysis and feedback, systematic data collection might be built into the policy initiative. This, if it is not too onerous — and clearly it must not be — might itself become a valuable management tool.

Finally, it was suggested that evaluation and feedback should become more than the 'learning by doing' process outlined above: that an explicitly *experimental* policy system should be established along the lines of the U.S. Department of Commerce's Experimental Technology Incentives Program

(ETIP). Here the policy system becomes itself part of a process of innovation. Whether or not public policy makers and administrators generally would wish to become, or are capable of becoming, part of such a system is another question entirely!

References

Coleman, J. S., (1972), *Policy Research in the Social Sciences,* Morristown, N. J., General Learning Press

de Leon, P., (1976), *A Cross-National Comparison of Nuclear Development Strategies,* Santa Monica, Ca., Rand Corporation

DTI, (1982), 'Evaluation of the United Kingdom's Department of Trade and Industry's Manufacturing Advisory Service', London, Technology Policy Division, Department of Trade and Industry

Farina, C. and Gibbons, M., (1979), 'A Quantitative Analysis of the SRC's Policy of Selectivity and Concentration', *Research Policy,* 7, 301 — 308

Gardiner, N., (1975), *Economics of Industrial Subsidies,* London, Department of Industry

Gibbons, M., (1982), 'The Evaluation of Government Policies for Innovation', paper presented to Six Countries Programme Workshop, Windsor, 22 — 23 November, 1982

Golding, A. M., (1978), 'The Influence of Government Procurement on the Development of the Semi-Conductor Industry in the U.S. and Britain', Six Countries Programme Workshop on Government Procurement Policies and Innovation, Dublin, Ireland (PO Box 215, Delft, The Netherlands)

Herbert, R. and Hoar, R. W., (1982), *Government and Innovation: Experimenating with Change,* ETIP, National Bureau of Standards, Washington, DC, November, Report No. NBS-GCR-ETIP 82-100

Hetman, F., (1983), 'The Evaluation of the Effectiveness of Government Measures for the Stimulation of Innovation', Paris, OECD, DSTI/SPR/83.40, May

Irvine, J., Martin, B., Pavitt, K. and Rothwell, R., (1981), *Government Support for Industrial Research in Norway,* A Science Policy Research Unit Report, University of Sussex, July

Kogan, M. et al (1980) 'Government's Commissioning of Research: a Case Study' (mimeo), University of Brunel, U.K.

Little, B., (1974), *The Role of Government in Assisting New Product Development,* School of Business Administration, University of Western Ontario, London, Canada. Working Paper Series No. 114, March

Meyer-Krahmer, F., Gielow, G. and Kuntze, U., (1983), Impacts of Government Incentives for Industrial Innovation, An Analysis of the Federal Programme Funding for R & D Personnel in the Federal Republic of Germany, Research Policy, 12.

Meyer-Krahmer, F., Gielow, G. and Kuntze, U. (1984): Wirkungsanalyse der Zuschuesse fuer Personal in Forschung und Entwicklung, Karlsruhe, Report for the Fraunhofer-Institut fuer Systemtechnik und Innovationsforschung (ISI), May 1984

Nelson, R. R., (1974), 'Intellectualising the Moon-Ghetto Metaphor: A Study of the Current Malaise of Rational Analysis in Social Problems', *Policy Sciences,* 5

Overmeer, W. and Prakke, F. (1978), *Government Procurement Policies and Industrial Innovation,* Six Countries Programme Secretariat, Delft.

Piatier, A., (1983), 'The Use of Surveys for Evaluating Innovation Policies', Paris, OECD, DSTI/SPR/83.41, May

Rothwell, R., (1982), *Evaluating the Effectiveness of Government Innovation Policy*, Six Countries Programme Report, Six Countries Secretariate, PO Box 215, TNO, 2600 AE Delft, The Netherlands.

Rothwell, R. and Zegveld, W., (1981), *Industrial Innovation and Public Policy*, Francis Pinter Ltd., London

Rothwell, R. and Zegveld, W., (1985), *Reindustrialisation and Technology*, Longman Press, London

CHAPTER 8

Venture Capitalism

G. Houttuin

Venture capital is a subject of much discussion in Europe. The venture capitalists of the U.S. are held up as an example to Europe and there is at least a suspicion that many policy makers or other interested parties feel that if only Europe had an equivalent venture capital industry, it could rise to a new level of innovative activity. Mr. Houttuin provided these notes on what is as yet a gap in the Six Countries Programme.

Mr. Guus Houttuin is a Policy Adviser in the Technology Policy Division of the Dutch Ministry of Economic Affairs. He is involved in the conduct of bilateral cooperation programmes and in the evaluation of other countries' innovation policies. He holds a Master's degree in International Law from the University of Amsterdam.

For the purpose of this chapter venture capital is regarded as being capital committed, as shareholdings, for the formation and start-up of small firms specialising in new ideas or new technologies. It is however not only an injection of funds into a new firm; it is also an input of the skills needed to set the firm up, organise and manage it and run its commercial activity. The main difference between passive classical investment and venture capital is that in the latter type of investment there is a continuous involvement on the part of the investor in the firm's development.

Venture capitalism covers four distinct types of financing, corresponding to four stages in a firm's life cycle.

l. Seeding finance.   In this stage the venture capitalist starts by financing the entrepreneur to develop specifications for the new product or service and to establish a business plan. The average American venture capitalist receives about 200 — 300 investment proposals a year. After the first analysis most of these proposals are turned down and it is estimated that of the remaining proposals about 70 per cent are abandoned at the end of the seeding phase.

2. Start-up finance.   This is the stage at which most venture capitalists become involved. The firm still has to be set up to produce a product or service and carry out the business plan. The management skills of the venture capitalist are called upon. The start-up phase normally takes about one year. As the risks are considerable, venture capitalists often spread the risks by finance-sharing.

3. Fledgling finance.   Product and service are on the market but the firm does not have an image or sales network. The main difficulty at this stage is the amount of funds needed, which explains why it is useful for several venture capitalists to be involved.

4. Establishment finance.   This is the stage at which the firm (in the case of the United States) enters the stock market. This is normally a quotation on the over-the-counter market, a market to which the conditions of admission are less stringent than at the regular stock market, especially relevant for small and medium sized firms. This is also the point at which venture capitalists realise the profit of their investment. Using the exit of the stock market they sell their wares, make capital gains (50 times the initial value is no exception) and by regaining new and larger funds can look around for new projects and new entrepreneurs.

These four stages generally take between five and ten years in the United States with an average investment of 5 — 700,000 dollars. An alternative and quicker exit mechanism is purchase by a large group even at the fledgling stage.

What is the rate of success in venture capitalism?

Twenty to 30 per cent of projects fail at an early stage and the funds invested are lost. Forty to 60 per cent never reach the stage of spectacular rise in value.

Some projects neither fail nor succeed. These projects are called 'walking deaths' with obviously little chance of capital gains.

There is however no reason for pessimism. About 20% of the projects account for the high return on investment of the venture capitalists. The rate of profit to venture capitalists thus varies considerably. The average rate of profit is put at between 30 and 60 per cent mainly by investing it in firms — or, more correctly, projects — like Atari, Apple, Digital Equipment, ROLM, Genetech etc.).

At present there are five main categories of operators in the venture capital market.

1. Individual venture capitalists.   These are individuals, including former heads of companies, who have sufficient funds and skills to risk their personal capital. They account for only a small part of the investment.

2. High technology mutual funds.   This is the most important category in the venture capital market. Each is funded by a number of partners (the so called 'Limited Partners') and is managed by partners who receive a commission on profits (the so called 'General Partners').

Most of the limited partners are traditional finance institutions e.g. pension funds. The fact that the most prominent venture capitalists use funds from the traditional finance institutions reflects the main feature of venture capitalism. It is more than the provision of high-risk capital in exchange for high returns; it is also the provision of special skills in identifying, evaluating and 'piloting' firms working with new technology.

A recent trend is that some of these high technology mutual funds become joint stock companies, with a market quotation.

By doing this they can get more capital and invest in more ventures to spread the risk.

Examples of these companies are: Merrill Lynch Venture Partners, Fidelity Technology Fund and Twentieth Century Ultra.

3. Small business investment companies – SBIC's. These companies are regulated and licensed by the Federal Government. They can borrow up to three times their capital from government and their role is to stimulate small business. The SBIC's have proven to be an excellent training ground for the first generation venture capitalists.

4. Investment banks. The venture capital activity of traditional banks is still limited.

5. Venture capital divisions and subsidiaries of major groups. Although primarily intra-company oriented these divisions and subsidiaries also invest in outside projects, provided they are relevant to the development and technological diversification of their group.

The users of venture capital

The users are people with an idea for a new product or service, but without the capital or the business know-how to bring it to fruition. As far as the U.S. economy is concerned the numbers of such entrepreneurs increased considerably during the last decade, due to two factors:

— the development of a whole range of new basic technologies (e.g. micro electronics, new materials, biotechnology) which has brought about new opportunities for innovation and new goods and services. As the basic technologies are easy to obtain (or buy) the opportunities for further development work are many;
— the economic crisis which has resulted in the major industrial groups slowing down their R & D activities to a

certain extent and concentrating their (limited) funds on specific projects. This has encouraged researchers to develop their work outside the parent company.

According to Bruce Merrifield, Assistant Secretary for Productivity, Technology and Innovation of the Department of Trade and Commerce, there is an enormous fund of unused scientific and technological knowledge. At the knowledge-end of venture capitalism the next decade probably will not bring any bottlenecks.

Some essential characteristics of venture capital investments:

— venture capital investments are a long-term activity, up to ten years;
— the venture capitalist is involved very actively in the enterprise in which he has invested. Besides his financial involvement in the newly established firm he brings in his managerial skills, specific experiences and contacts. Apart from being one of the main characteristics of venture capitalism this managerial involvement is one of the reasons, at least in the United States, for the high growth and success of the venture capital market. As to the management capabilities of the firm itself, most venture capitalists seem to prefer a good management and an 'average' product to a combination of 'average' management and a good product;
— venture capitalists more often invest in new uses for already existing technologies than in research and development of new technologies.

Initiatives outside the United States

The spread of venture capitalism is a largely North American phenomenon. A number of venture capital schemes have been launched in other OECD countries, especially during the early seventies, but none seems to have really succeeded. In the last three years there has been a revival in ideas and initiatives for the development of venture capital markets.

This development stems from two considerations:

— most policy makers are of the opinion that it is impossible to have dynamic high tech industries without autonomous and innovative SMEs;
— it seems fairly impossible for these SMEs to develop without a sound venture capital market, because there is hardly a substitute for venture capital as a source of funds and management skills for new technology firms.

The *United Kingdom* seems to have been the most successful. In 1980 an 'Unlisted Securities Market' was set up in London. As pointed out earlier an over-the-counter stock market is one of the preconditions for venture capital development. Already several private venture capital companies have been formed, as well as a 'British Venture Capital Association'.

Most of the *Japanese* venture capital companies are subsidiaries of the major finance institutions. The Tokyo over-the-counter market is considered to have conditions for admission which are too strict for high technology starters. At the same time the conservative attitude of the venture capitalists makes the Japanese venture capital market a less spectacular one than the North American, albeit with some striking results, especially in the sector of informatics, computers and communication.

As in the United Kingdom and Japan, *France* has public funds and agencies which are to act as private venture capital companies. Although a government support scheme for private venture capitalists is available and an over-the-counter market has been created, French venture capitalism is still in its childhood.

In Germany, the promotion of venture capital started with the formation of the Venture Capital Society (Wagnis-finanzierungsgesellschaft) in 1975, an investment company of 29 leading German banks that operated with a state guarantee for losses. This company ceased its operations in 1984 and started again as a completely private venture capital and venture management company. In 1983, an experimental federal programme (DM 325 m.) to support new technology based firms was launched that aims at assisting and stimulating a venture capital market in West Germany.

As a result the first private venture capital firms started their operations in 1983. By the end of 1984, approximately 30 firms were offering management services and venture capital, amounting to about DM 750 m.

The possibilities for young firms to go public are not comparable to the over-the-counter-markets in the U.S. or in the U.S.A.

Sweden has some interesting results with the extra tax deduction for shares in new companies.

In the *Netherlands* there exists, since 1981, a state guarantee scheme for the participation in new firms by officially recognised venture capital companies (the so called 'Particuliere Participatiemaatschappijen'). Together with the creation of an over-the-counter market this scheme has been a positive incentive for the development of the Dutch venture capital market. At the moment government is considering tax-deduction measures for private persons acquiring new shares.

The internationalisation of venture capitalism is a well known fact. One only has to think of all the European investments in the United States. In this aspect a remarkable European initiative was taken in June 1984. Ten leading European companies founded a limited liability company in Amsterdam which will invest venture capital in new high-tech companies. 'Euroventures' with large enterprises like Philips, Volvo, Fiat, Olivetti and Bosch will have a starting capital of $33 m. The establishment of this venture capital company in Amsterdam will probably also have positive effects on the Dutch venture capital market. Among the reasons for establishing the company in the Netherlands were the good stock market climate and the fiscal system.

Also in the spring of 1984 a European Venture Capital Association (EVCA) has been founded mainly as a discussion forum.

Some tentative conclusions

The role of venture capital varies from country to country. It is important in the United States, and in Europe really only in the United Kingdom. Sweden and the Netherlands seem to have made a reasonably good start but the rest of Europe is still lagging behind. In the light of the several national initiatives to stimulate the development of the venture capital market some comments can be made:

— the venture capital market is not cut off from other finance markets: upstream it is funded largely by the traditional financial institutions and downstream it needs the existence of active stock markets which allow venture capitalists to exit and reinject their funds in new projects. Plans for the support of national venture capital markets call for a development or adjustment of the other financial markets as well;

— establishing a national stock of managerial skills in the evaluation and commercial piloting of small high tech firms is probably a longer and more critical process than the creation of a capital influx;

— state venture capital companies may suffer from the use of non-commercial criteria while running their business. There is an obvious risk that they may turn into ordinary government support organisations;

— venture capital needs entrepreneurial dynamism to develop, which is to a large extent a socio-cultural phenomenon and therefore difficult to grasp;

— also the entrepreneurs must be willing to accept 'outside' interference i.e. other shareholders and managers.

The Six Countries Programme

The Six Countries Programme on Aspects of Government Policies towards Technological Innovation in Industry is an international study, started in March 1975.

The original participants came from four countries — the Netherlands, West Germany, France, and U.K. — and were later joined by Ireland and Canada (in 1975), Belgium and Sweden (in 1981), and Austria in 1984.

The members meet twice yearly and it has been the practice to collect the proceedings of these workshops for publication. Copies can be obtained from The Secretariat of the Programme at Dfl 50 each.

Six Countries Programme on Aspects of Government Policies towards Technological Innovation in Industry Workshops

1. Government direct financial assistance to industry, programmes, experiences and trends (12 — 13 October 1976: London)
2. Government aid to technical change in the mechanical engineering industries (19 April 1977: Karlsruhe)
3. The current international economic climate and policies for technical innovation (November 1977)
4. Small and medium sized manufacturing firms: their role and problems in innovation, government policy in Europe, the USA, Canada, Japan and Israel (21 — 22 November 1977: The Hague)
5. Government procurement policies and industrial innovation (6 — 7 June 1978: Dublin)
6. Technical change and employment (13 — 14 November 1978: Paris)
7. Industrial innovation and government regulation (11 — 13 June 1979: The Hague)
8. Trends in collective industrial research (26 — 27 November 1979: London)
9. National innovation policies (1 — 2 December 1980: Berlin)
10. New entrepreneurship and the smaller innovative firm (9 — 10 June 1980: Limerick)
11. Regional innovation policy: technology policies or regional policies (1 — 2 June 1981: Sophia Antipolis)

12. A systematic approach to innovation (23 — 24 November 1981: The Hague)
13. Industry university relations (10 — 11 May 1982: Stockholm)
14. Evaluating the effectiveness of government innovation policies (22 — 23 November 1982: London)
15. Technological culture and success in industry (6 — 7 June 1983: Paris)
16. Technological information from abroad: scientific attaches and other public institutions, industrial needs and public policies (December 1983: The Hague)
17. Policies for industrial innovation — situation and perspectives (7 — 8 May 1984: Bonn)
18. Regional innovation policies and programmes (19 — 20 November 1984: Limerick)

Index